Case Studies in
Music Education

Case Studies in Music Education

Frank Abrahams
Westminster Choir College of Rider University

Paul Head
University of Delaware

GIA Publications, Inc.
Chicago

4MAT, Excel, Learning Type Measure (LTM) and Hemispheric Mode Indicator (HMI) are federally registered trademarks of Excel, Inc.

Excerpts from My *Fair Lady* © The Estate of Alan Jay Lerner. Used with permission.

This book is dedicated with love and appreciation to
our families:

Carol, Andrew, Laura, and Katie Head,
and to
Ellen, Daniel, and Emily Abrahams.

The authors wish to thank Margaret Jones for her help with the
preparation of the manuscript; Jason Iannuzzi and Traci Maher
for their careful proofreading; Daniel Abrahams for his candid
critiques; Emily Abrahams for her help with the graphics and
layout; Ellen Abrahams for her love and support; and Carol
Head for being a great sounding board and having the ability to
always "see the other side."

Finally, we wish to extend our appreciation to our students at
Westminster Choir College of Rider University and the
University of Delaware who provided thoughtful comments and
criticisms. This book is for them, too.

Table of Contents

Introduction

Each chapter in this text is based on an eight-step teaching model, known as the 4MAT® System, developed by Bernice McCarthy and articulated in her books *The 4MAT System: Teaching to Learning Styles Using Left/Right Preferences* and *About Learning*. Each chapter includes a case study where the student encounters a situation typical of those faced by music teachers in the daily execution of their teaching responsibilities. In addition to the pedagogical issues that provide the centerpiece of the case, each case includes a moral dilemma. The authors believe that because teaching involves the resolution of ethical issues every day, it is important to include such situations in the context of music education courses. It is these issues that often cause new teachers the most discomfort. The purpose of each case study is to present a problem that will generate and stimulate discussion cooperatively in small groups or as a class in total. The activities are designed to connect the problems of the case to the issues presented in each chapter. Information needed to solve the problem provides opportunities for students to practice and apply what they have learned. Finally, students develop a plan of action. It is suggested that instructors provide time in each chapter for students to share their action plans and to teach each other.

Just as form provides structure and organization to various musical genres, we have borrowed the labels—introduction, exposition, development, improvisation and recapitulation—to sequence the presentation of material in each chapter. Although the reader may feel that the terms loosely apply, they give each chapter a uniform structure. At the beginning of each chapter, advanced organizers introduce the reader to what is to come. The content of the case study presents the problem by exposing the music education and moral issues. Included in this segment is time for process and analysis through discussion. The ideas are developed through the exploration of information which the student needs to resolve the conflict and solve the problem of the case. Students then add something of their own by improvising and thereby creating their own solutions. In the final section, the students and their teacher have the opportunity to recap, refine, refocus, and tune their work. It is important to point out that within each of the large sections (i.e., exposition, development, improvisation, and recapitulation), there are two sub-sections. One sub-section is designed to appeal to left mode approaches to learning, the other right mode; that is, the use of analysis and synthesis in some mixture of relevance and balance. It is the intention of the authors that all students do all sections of each chapter since the goal is to use the whole brain. The modalities are arranged according to the order set out by Bernice McCarthy:

Exposition
    A. Right Mode
    B. Left Mode
Development
    A. Right Mode
    B. Left Mode
Improvisation
    A. Left Mode
    B. Right Mode

Recapitulation
- A. Left Mode
- B. Right Mode

It is hoped that, consistent with McCarthy's research findings, students at particular points through the material will find their learning "comfort zone" as well as necessitating stretching into their less comfortable places. By honoring the various comfort zones, students will find the chapters to be meaningful, purposeful, and helpful to their teaching and learning.

The cases in this book may be used in tandem with a teaching methods textbook in a music methodology class or by themselves in a music education seminar at the undergraduate or graduate level. The authors hope that they stimulate discussion, provoke thought, and bridge the gap between theory and practice. Most importantly, we hope that they generate an excitement and enthusiasm for music teaching and music learning.

Frank Abrahams
Paul Head
March, 1998

From the Authors

It should be helpful to the reader to know that *Case Studies in Music Education* is actually an outgrowth not of an idea for a book, but of an attempt to make the process of teaching teachers more meaningful and efficient. With the increasing emphasis in the University community on teaching critical thinking skills while addressing the needs of diverse learners, it has become abundantly clear that the traditional "lecture approach" is no longer sufficient if we are to create active learners in our own classrooms, let alone the future classrooms of our students.

The idea of becoming an active learner means that we must require our students to take a vested interest in the matter at hand. That is to somehow present material in a way that makes it relevant to their lives and creates within each person a desire to "solve the problem." To be sure, there are few absolutes in teaching methodology. The acquisition of pedagogical tools and a working knowledge thereof is essential, of course, but at some point in the process, each individual teacher must make a series of decisions that will reflect that particular teacher's strengths in the classroom as well as his or her personal philosophy in regard to the subject matter.

The most valuable attribute of each case study that follows is the fact that the authors often found themselves with opposing perspectives when faced with solving the ethical dilemmas in each case. The fact is that there are no definitive solutions to most of the issues presented in this book. The emphasis here is not the solution, but the process. As students gain experience they come to realize that there are viable approaches to nearly every obstacle, and one must embrace a two-fold process in becoming a master teacher; that of identifying one's own personal philosophy of music education, and of recognizing traits which are good in someone else's style.

When dealing with each case students are encouraged to present varying perspectives and develop rational support based on what they believe. It is this struggle that has made these cases so very useful for each of the authors, as well as enriching for each of their students.

Analyzing a Case Study

The case studies in this book describe a particular situation where at least one of the participants faces a dilemma. That person is forced to make a decision and to plan a course of action. The characters in a case are called the actors. Those affected in the case are called the stakeholders. For example, if a case were about Mr. Finch, the school principal, assigning Miss Jones, the music teacher, to lunchroom duty three days per week, Mr. Finch and Miss Jones would be the actors. The children in the lunchroom would be the stakeholders. Facts in the body of the case might include school rules. For example, children must be supervised in the lunchroom, and all teachers in the building are assigned turns on a rotating schedule. The dilemma might center around Miss Jones wanting to work with children who needed help matching pitch during lunch instead of doing the lunchroom duty while Mr. Finch insists on her doing the duty. The action Miss Jones takes—that is, fighting the assignment or accepting the assignment and finding another time to work with her students—presents the dilemma. The facts of the case involve the location of the school, the socioeconomic status of the children, the school rules (i.e. Do all teachers have a special assignment such as lunchroom duty?), and so forth.

There are two ways to analyze the case studies in this book.

In the first method, identify the actors. Include all of the information you are given about each one. Then, identify the stakeholders. Sometimes it is necessary to include stakeholders who may not be mentioned in the specific case but who are still affected. For instance, in the case of lunchroom duty the school custodians are most definitely stakeholders. If there are no teachers doing lunchroom duty they might have to do the duty or perform a more extensive cleanup. Next, list all of the facts. What information are you given? Summarize the dilemma. Then brainstorm possible solutions or alternative plans of action. Remember that there are always options. Problems always have more than one solution. Finally, choose the best solution for the situation.

Example One:
  I. The Actors
     A. Mr. Finch, school principal responsible for the safety of children in his building, including during lunch.
     B. Miss Jones, music teacher who wishes to provide extra help for her children during the lunch period.
  II. The Stakeholders
     A. Mr. Finch and Miss Jones.
     B. The children in the school.
     C. The custodians who have to clean up after lunch.
     D. The other teachers in the building who take their turns supervising the lunchroom.
  III. The Facts
     A. Mr. Finch has assigned Miss Jones to supervise the lunchroom three times each week.
     B. Miss Jones wants to use the lunch time to work with children who are having difficulty matching pitch.
  IV. The Dilemma
     A. If Miss Jones refuses to do the lunchroom duty, she could be reprimanded by Mr. Finch. On the other hand, if she does do the lunchroom duty, she will neglect her students who need her help.

B. If Mr. Finch excuses Miss Jones from lunchroom duty, he will have a staff morale issue on his hands. He could be accused of playing favorites and not being fair to the other teachers.

V. Possible Solutions

A. Miss Jones could do her lunchroom duty and find another time to work with her students.

B. Mr. Finch could volunteer to cover for Miss Jones one day each week so that she could work with her students.

C. Miss Jones could trade duties with another teacher. Instead of lunchroom duty, Miss Jones could do after school bus duty and early morning school yard duty while a colleague could do her lunchroom supervision.

A second way to analyze a case study is to create a mindmap. A mindmap is a visual representation of an outline. Draw an oval in the center of a piece of 11 x 17 drawing paper. Inside the oval summarize the dilemma. Then around the oval place the actors and the stakeholders. Draw lines from the actors and the stakeholders to the dilemma and draw lines that connect specific actors to specific stakeholders. List the facts of the case along the upper parameter of the drawing paper, then brainstorm solutions and place them on the outer parameters along the lower portion of the drawing paper. Draw lines connecting the actors and the stakeholders to each suggested solution. This provides a visual representation or map of the case. Star the solution that you think is the best one.

Best solution: Your choice!

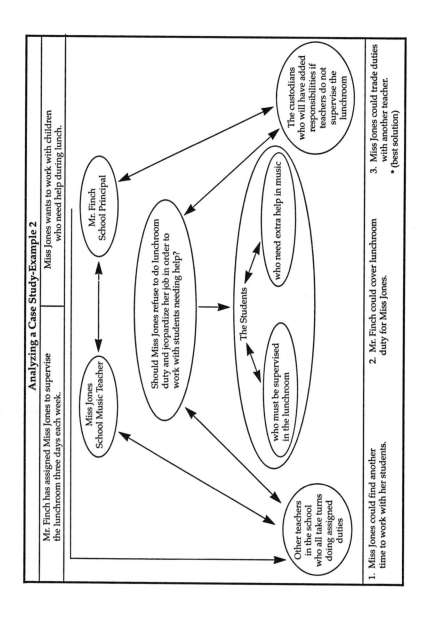

Analyzing a Case Study-Example 2

Mr. Finch has assigned Miss Jones to supervise the lunchroom three days each week.	Miss Jones wants to work with children who need help during lunch.

Miss Jones
School Music Teacher

Mr. Finch
School Principal

The custodians who will have added responsibilities if teachers do not supervise the lunchroom

Should Miss Jones refuse to do lunchroom duty and jeopardize her job in order to work with students needing help?

The Students

who need extra help in music

who must be supervised in the lunchroom

Other teachers in the school who all take turns doing assigned duties

1. Miss Jones could find another time to work with her students.

2. Mr. Finch could cover lunchroom duty for Miss Jones.

3. Miss Jones could trade duties with another teacher.
* (best solution)

Solitude of Success

Introduction

Particularly at the secondary level, many music teachers will find recruitment to be an important and necessary part of their job. While most schools are forced to "pick and choose" between the electives they are able to offer, decisions are frequently made on the basis of the enrollment for each particular class. One might look at it as a process of supply and demand: if enough students insist on taking a particular class, the school administration will often respond by adding another section.

First-year teacher Michael Davidson found this to be true while building his first job into a full-day schedule of music classes. His strategy was not simply one of numbers, but an effort to build a comprehensive choral program that would meet the needs of his students at each individual level. What he did not consider was that for every cause, there is an effect. Even before the first students were to show up for instruction, Michael was already feeling alienated from his colleagues, largely a victim of his own success.

Exposition

A. Read the Case: *Solitude of Success*

Mr. Davidson was feeling smug as he left the principal's office one balmy July afternoon. Here it was already midsummer, and most of his friends were still out beating the pavement looking for a job. Michael Davidson was elated about his new position as the choral director at Jefferson High School.

Michael Davidson suspected that he was given the job largely due to his outgoing personality. Apparently, the previous choir director had been "less than successful." Jefferson had once been regionally famous for its outstanding choirs, but nobody appeared too interested in singing anymore.

Michael didn't really believe this could be true, and he voiced his opinion in the interview. The panel was eager to hear his ideas for recruitment and how he would restore the Jefferson choirs to their original fame and stature.

The remainder of the summer was anything but restful for the enthusiastic young teacher. There were phone calls to make and students to meet. Before the first day of school, he would tap every available resource looking for yet one more way to draw new interest in the Jefferson choirs. If Davidson was successful, the principal had vowed to add another class section to accommodate choir enrollment of over 140 students. This would allow Davidson to begin a men's ensemble to parallel the training available in Treble Choir. He thought this to be crucial if he was to develop the type of training that would ensure the longevity of his program. However, such goals were all but impossible given the 87 students currently enrolled for the coming semester.

Tuesday, September 3rd was the first of two in-service days that routinely marked the beginning of the school year. On this day, many teachers would report to campus for the first time since last June, but Michael had practically been living in the music building for the past month and a half working to recruit, audition, and entice the students of Jefferson High School. In the end, the time seemed to have been well spent. He needed to check with the registrar, but he was sure he was approaching the quota that would guarantee him another section of choir.

As he walked on campus toward the main office he happened upon Roger Parker, the veteran band director. "Good morning, Mr. Parker!" Michael was eager to find a good friend in this new colleague.

Mr. Parker disregarded the ritual of a gratuitous greeting. "It seems that a number of students want to drop out of band. Would you know anything about that?" Mr. Parker questioned aggressively.

"Uh . . . gee. . . no . . . I don't think so. Why do you ask?" Michael thought that he knew why, but at the moment, ignorance seemed the best policy.

"Well, it seems they've decided to take choir instead of band, and they don't have enough class options to do both," Mr. Parker continued.

"Well . . . I . . . think you'd better send them back to talk to me. There must be some misunderstanding." Mr. Davidson had not told the students to drop out of band; he was just trying to build up their interest in the choir.

"Well, for two of the three it's already too late." Mr. Parker was annoyed. "They have already been to see their counselors. You might consider staying in your own court, Mr. Davidson." Michael understood Mr. Parker's anger; but at the same time, he felt it was largely Parker's own fault. If students didn't want to drop band, then they wouldn't do it.

As Michael Davidson entered the main office in search of the registrar, Allen Whitworth, the vice principal, spotted him first. "Mr. Davidson, come into my office for a moment. I've got great news for you!" Michael came in and sat down as the vice principal continued, "The numbers are in! We've gone ahead and scheduled that boy's chorus you wanted. You need to go see Martha in the registrar's office with updated lists right away." Michael was thrilled. He thanked the vice-principal profusely as he hurried across the office to reap the fruit of his labors. School had not yet even begun, and he was already feeling like a success story. The altercation with Roger Parker, the band teacher, had already lost its sting.

A few hours later Michael Davidson attended his first faculty luncheon. While he had met seemingly hundreds of students, he was still a stranger to most of the faculty. As he worked his way down the serving table of catered lasagna and green salad, he couldn't help but overhear the distressed teacher across the table relive the agony and frustrations of her morning to anyone willing to listen. Enrollment in her ceramic classes had dropped, and she had been informed just this morning that she would either be forced to teach in another department, or she would be cut back to four-fifths time. This is all due to the new guy in the music department.

Suddenly it occurred to Michael what was happening. He abandoned his plate and bolted out the door toward the vice principal's office to find out the rest of the story. Barely outside, he found himself face to face with Mr. Whitworth. "You didn't tell me someone was going to lose their job!" Michael was somewhere between panic and concern.

"Lose their job?" Mr. Whitworth was puzzled. "What are you talking about?"

"Did you make cuts in someone else's schedule in order to add the Men's Ensemble?" Michael sounded almost accusing.
"Not exactly, Michael," assured Whitworth. "It's more like a redistribution."

"Redistribution?" the young teacher replied.

"Not to worry. Just do the math. There are only so many students, and X number of class sections. If you see more students, someone else sees less. It's as simple as that."

"So it is my fault!" Michael seemed stunned by the realization.

"Just do your job Mr. Davidson. That's why we hired you."

B. Consider the following questions:

1. What exactly is the nature of Michael's dilemma? How should he prioritize the needs of his program in regard to his interaction with other faculty and the school community? What

are the possible ramifications of his recent success?

2. What are the factors he must consider in order to create a win/win situation for students and faculty alike?

Development

A. In small groups, write new lyrics to a familiar tune that summarize Michael Davidson's dilemma. The first verse should be about all his hard work recruiting students. The second verse should focus on the unexpected ramifications of his efforts.

B. The complexities of this case revolve around how one sees himself or herself in the role of the music teacher. Some people will focus nearly all their energy on the students as they feel that their purpose is to facilitate learning and to create a meaningful musical experience. These people are extremely dedicated and will go to any extreme to provide opportunities for their students and ensembles. However, others will come to realize quite early on that students come and students go, and if they are to remain in the teaching profession for any period of time, they will need to make friends and acquaintances, essential to the lasting community of the school. There is an old adage that states, "Be sure to make friends with the person that runs the school—the principal's secretary." This is neither bad advice nor is it conclusive within itself. You will find that many of your goals as a music teacher will only be attainable if you enable the faculty and administration to embrace your values as a teacher and your priorities as a professional. In an effort to disentangle the perplexities of Mr. Davidson's dilemma, this chapter will discuss three separate elements of which one must be aware as an effective member of a cohesive faculty. These are creating the master schedule, recruiting students for the music program, and creating and maintaining healthy relationships with your colleagues.

The process of creating a master schedule for a comprehensive secondary school is much more complicated than it might seem. Often there will be one administrator on campus whose chief responsibility is to design and maintain the scheduling and registration process. It is useful to meet with this person before school begins so that you understand how the registration process operates and what the appropriate procedures will be as you enlist students for your classes.

An important realization in this process is that public schools are funded by the government on the basis of how many students are in attendance at a particular school site at any given time. (Similarly, private schools are driven by tuition producing enrollment.) It is not uncommon for a school site to open under-staffed, giving the administrator the opportunity to see how many students "actually show up" before making final hiring decisions and adjustments to the master schedule. If you are for-tunate enough to be teaching in a district with increasing enroll-ments, this will usually mean mayhem for the first few weeks of school as students are shuffled from class to class while new fac-ulty is added and classroom space is created. Once attendance figures have stabilized and additional faculty have been hired, the administration can make the final adjustments that keep hundreds of students each on an individual plan that must always prove successful in meeting the individual's needs and course requirements. Since the school receives funding only for those students that are in regular attendance, and it is this fund-ing that finances the budget for the entire school operation, you will find the keeping of accurate and thorough attendance records to be of paramount importance to the school administra-tion. They will know that they are allocated X number of dollars for each day each student is at school. Multiply the number of students by an average of 180 school days within a year and this will give you the figure that will be allotted to keep a school fully operational for a fiscal year.

Perhaps a case study within a case study will be most helpful here. Jefferson High School anticipates an enrollment of 600 stu-dents on opening day of the coming school year. As the contract with the teachers' association mandates a maximum class size of 25 students within a six-period day, this will allow the administration to offer up to 144 individual course listings, assuming every desk in every classroom is utilized every period. For example, 600 students each taking 6 classes equals 3600 placements, divided by 25 students in each class results in 144 course offerings. One week into the school year, the enrollment stabilizes at 650 students, which allows the administration to add two more class sections that best meet the needs of the collective student body. In this case, Mr. Davidson would have been able to add two classes without having an adverse effect elsewhere on campus. But what if the school was declining in enrollment, and the student body shrinks to 575 students? Mr. Davidson may be asked to give up one of his "elective" classes even though enrollment in the music program has remained consistent or even increased. Recent trends in the mandating of fine art requirements at the state and district levels have helped somewhat in keeping music courses as part of the core curriculum, but the reality is that elective classes will always be eliminated before a school cuts a course that is specifically required for graduation and/or college entrance prerequisites.

An additional irony here is that teaching contracts in many districts will have special provisions for fine arts and physical education teachers allowing them to exceed the maximum class size. Imagine if the marching band teacher was only allowed to have 25 students in the marching band and drill units. Some schools boast performance ensembles of well over 100 students. Given the above case at Jefferson High School, this would help give the administration additional flexibility since the music teacher may have a single performance group equivalent to the entire course load of a teacher in another department. In such cases, it is possible for a music teacher to negotiate an additional class section such as theory, or a beginning instruments class that may only have eight or ten students. This is offset by the large numbers taught in the performance groups that meet at other times during the day.

Of course, there are many other considerations that the administration will have to deal with in the building of the master schedule. Many singleton offerings will never reach maximum quotas. Honors classes, remedial classes, calculus, regional industrial and agriculture offerings, and special education courses will all be necessary to provide a comprehensive education within a given school environment but will seldom reach capacity due to the specific nature of the subject area. However, the task at hand for the effective music educator is to gain an understanding and empathy for how scheduling decisions are made and how one must be an advocate for music as an integral part of the curriculum and the school community. When dealing with administration, represent yourself in a light that will be advantageous to their agenda as well as your own. Know the policies for preregistration and scheduling of classes and adhere to the rules. You will always find success more attainable when you are perceived as a team player who is willing to embrace broader goals which serve the needs of the students beyond those of the music program.

There are many methods books available that will suggest numerous strategies and approaches to recruitment for school music programs. In addition, the small group work as related to the analysis of this case should likewise generate some helpful ideas. The recruitment issues as related to *this* case are a bit more broad based. The pervading question is, how do your goals and strategies for building a lasting music program relate to the overall design for the school?

In recent years, many schools have adopted "mission statements" in an effort to clearly identify what a student should have achieved once he or she has successfully completed the twelfth grade. Many districts take such pride in this declaration that it will be posted at every school in the district, usually in the main office where parents can be reaffirmed that their children are receiving the educational opportunities they deserve. An adept music teacher will make a point of becoming familiar with such district policies and work on building their own program upon one or more of the premises therein. For instance, those mission statements that expressly advocate a well-rounded education in the arts and sciences give an opportunistic music teacher a direct lead-in. If the mission of the district includes creating opportunities for every student to be successful in their own unique or individual way, this also will be an excellent platform on which to build any fine arts program. The ability to be creative in adapting such generalized statements will be of much use when designing and defending your philosophy and approach.

Mr. Davidson spent a great deal of time getting to know potential students upon his arrival at Jefferson High School. But he apparently made little effort to get to know his colleagues within the district or even at his own school site. He might have also spent some time with other music teachers in the district who have a better sense of local traditions and expectations. Likewise, stopping by other classrooms on campus while teachers in other subject areas are preparing for the coming term is an excellent way to become acquainted with other teachers before the confusion of the first day of school sets in. It is best to establish a reputation as *a person* lest people first come to know you for your entrepreneurial tendencies. Then, if you inadvertently become involved in a controversial issue later on, at least the initial interaction with other faculty members will not have been negative in character.

With "school choice" becoming an option in many districts around the country, it may also be wise to get a sense of the propriety within a given district or region. "School choice" is a program that is among the most recent solutions to desegregation, particularly in suburban areas that are adjacent to neighborhoods that are suffering from the challenges and social conditions of the inner city. This program will allow a student to enroll in any school in the district as long as transportation can be provided to and from the school site. A parallel program will frequently create "magnet" schools that offer specialized opportunities in areas like business and fine and industrial arts. This creates an entirely new dimension for the music teacher eager to build a successful program. Now, instead of functioning within a clearly delineated zone that regulates which students must attend which school, an assertive recruiter can search the entire district for suitable applicants for a growing empire. However, a word of caution is imperative here. Whether the current status of zones and boundaries is perceived, real or even obsolete, drawing on students that would otherwise attend other schools will not be helpful in building a reputation as a team player, especially if the incoming student is a strong musician. Creating an atmosphere of fierce competition between music teachers makes the workplace much more stressful for everyone involved and tends to de-emphasize the very essence of meaningful musical endeavors.

After the school year is under way and class sizes attain stability, there is a tendency to once again become caught up with the overwhelming responsibilities of administering a music program. With music to purchase, file, and distribute; instruments to check out and maintain, private lessons, faculty meetings, mailings to parents, and innumerable other responsibilities, it requires great self-discipline to actually leave the music building and interact with anyone else on campus. Failing to do so, however, will perpetuate the situation as you will end up assuming more and more responsibilities since you remain virtually anonymous as a member of the faculty. Take time to eat in the lunch room. Make a point of attending faculty meetings and serving on committees for the improvement of the school. Become involved in projects that don't have direct implications for the music program but that simply create a more pleasant environment for the faculty and student body at large. While it seems that there is never enough time for these additional commitments, this is a reality of being an integral member of the school community. Others will be more likely to come to the rescue when assistance is needed with music department projects—like chaperoning backstage or helping with the spring musical—if you have likewise been a resource for them. It is also worth noting that students often sign up for a music program due to its successful image. Other teachers will feel the same way. Many are eager to see students they teach in other subject areas meeting success as young musicians, too. It is human nature to want to be involved in something that is successful and which makes the school look good; but this cannot be attained by working in a vacuum. Think of it as cooperative learning on a grand scale, or perhaps even cooperative teaching.

Finally, and perhaps most importantly, be sincere. If colleagues have a sense they are being used or manipulated, the end result will be much worse than if they didn't know you at all. Once again, developing a sense of long-term goals for your role in the profession will be most useful here. A simple test might be, "once the students are gone, is there anyone left to talk to?" In addition, nurturing lasting relationships on the faculty can help make things tolerable when going through periods of frustration in the classroom. Hence, you will come to rely on your colleagues as they will come to rely upon you. This, in turn, will facilitate the role not only of a professional musician but of a professional *teacher* as well.

Improvisation

A. What strategies and ideas will Michael want to employ in building a music program while fostering effective relationships with his colleagues? In small groups, brainstorm to create two lists: one with ideas for effective recruiting, the other with considerations for school community public relations.

B. Design a recruitment brochure that can be sent to parents and students new to the school. Come up with a "sound bite" or slogan that will attract attention to your program. The Army used "Be all that you can be." CocaCola uses "It's the real thing." Your slogan should be the focus of the brochure. Share brochures with your classmates.

or

Design a web page for your ensemble. Be as creative as you wish. You might include links to your ensemble handbook or recent programs. You may wish to include a link "For Parents Only" describing how they might support their children's musical activities. The sky is truly the limit. Have fun.

Recapitulation

A. Critique recruitment brochures. Revise as necessary.

B. Role-play the interaction between Mr. Davidson and Mr. Parker, the disgruntled band teacher. Be prepared to cite not only those things you do to attract students, but how you are working for the school as a whole as well.

Up the Creek
without a Paddle

Introduction

Principals want teachers who are team players. Because site-based management is very popular, it is often the school principal rather than a music supervisor to whom the music teacher reports. It is important, therefore, that the music teacher earns the respect of the principal. For music programs to be valued, music teachers need the support of the school administration. Latisha Thomas has several issues to resolve in the following case. She must show the principal that she is concerned for the greater good of the school and that she is a good citizen of the school. On the other hand, she must be sure that her program is not being devalued or that she is being taken advantage of for the sake of an easy solution to a building problem. It is a fine line that any teacher walks in situations such as described in this case. For a new teacher, it is extremely difficult.

Exposition

A. Consider the issues in *Up the Creek Without a Paddle*
It is the first day of school. One week ago Latisha Thomas

was hired as the elementary specialist at Camelot Elementary School. When she interviewed for the position, they promised her the moon: plenty of resources, state of the art audio equipment, new music series, Orff instruments, and a freshly painted music room.

Yesterday she received a call from Mrs. Cox, the principal, informing her that there was a flood in one of the kindergarten rooms and that they needed her music room this week for the kindergarten classes. She must travel from room to room to teach her classes this week. Latisha looked over her lesson plans and adjusted her lesson content appropriately. She had planned to do some "get acquainted" activities anyway and she felt that she could manage without her own room for the first week. She did plan to use some CDs that her predecessor had purchased as well as resources from the new music series. She was very excited.

When Latisha arrived at school this morning she found that all of her equipment, resources, and materials had been packed up and moved to central storage. The first class, third grade, was to begin in one hour. Latisha panicked. What will she do? A thousand thoughts ran through her mind. She wanted to make a good impression, and yet how could she? And what about the principal? Why didn't she tell Latisha that she would not have access to any equipment or resources? Why didn't she ask Latisha what she needed for the week before she had everything packed away? Doesn't she value music education? Aren't the music classes as important as the kindergarten? Why did *she* have to be inconvenienced? Is it because she is the new kid on the block or because no one really cares about music in that school, or (and this was her worst fear) is it because she is young, female, and black?

B. Before discussing the issues of the case with your classmates, write your own feelings on a blank piece of paper. How would you react in this situation? Have you ever been or suspected that you have been the victim of discrimination?

Development

A. Divide a piece of drawing paper in half. On the left side draw a child who is the victim of stereotyping. On the right side draw a picture of a child who has no musical education in school. Use markers, crayons, or colored pencils. Compare the two children. Explain your drawings to the other members of your class. Discuss your findings.

B. Fighting stereotypes is an uphill battle. As music teachers in schools, we often feel undervalued and unappreciated. Most are overworked. Many schools provide music instruction with specialists so that classroom teachers can have a planning time or a break. Rarely does the music teacher have scheduled planning time and sometimes the music teacher does not even have a lunch break equal to that of the other teachers in the building. Some of this is our own fault. Sometimes we schedule extra rehearsals or group lessons or special projects during our lunch break and preparation period. Sometimes music rooms are located in such a remote part of the school building that it is hard to get to the lunchroom, eat, and be back in the classroom with enough time to set up for the next class.

It is important, however, to remember that music teachers are citizens of the school community. It is important to spend time with the other teachers in the building as much as is possible. Do not schedule activities with students during preparation or lunch periods. Take that time to interact with the other adults in your building. Make friends and work on your professional relationships. When it comes time for your concert programs, you will need the support of your colleagues in the building. When it comes time for children to select courses for the next year, you will need the support of the guidance counselors and those who set the schedule and assign students to courses.

Music teachers often balk when they are assigned a homeroom or are scheduled for recess, lunch, or bus duty. Somehow they feel that because they are specialists, they are special as well. This does not sit well with the other teachers and administrators in the building. Everyone must do their fair share. The responsibility for quality schools is everyone's responsibility. Maybe it is better to have fewer special groups so that the teacher has time to make a fair contribution to the management of the school.

Like many in our society, some principals feel that music is not important. They remember the music programs when they were children in school. Unfortunately, these are not always pleasant memories. Their perceptions are often that they had no real or lasting value. Many of these administrators attended school at a time when music was considered co-curricular or a "worthy use of leisure time," a popular notion in the 1960s and 1970s. Educational priorities changed radically in the 1950s and 1960s in an effort to meet the challenges of competition with the Soviet Union to be leaders in space, science, and technology. The publication of "A Nation at Risk" by the National Commission on Excellence in Education in 1983 confirmed that unless Americans did something drastic, they would be left behind. Schools began to enrich science and mathematics programs at the expense of music and the other arts. What schools did not realize, however, was that music and the other arts contributed to increased performance in many other academic areas including science and mathematics. Music teaches children to think creatively and to find multiple solutions to various problems. This is the kind of thinking one needs for complex mathematical and scientific operations. One also needs these skills to be a leader in business and industry. In other words, if schools want to raise achievement in the so-called "academic disciplines" or the "core subjects," they need strong arts programs. Music programs are valued when they connect to the goals of the schools. Music teachers are valued when they view themselves not as specialists on the fringe, but as integral contributors to the school family.

Women and minorities have not always been treated fairly. Women have found it harder to move up the career ladder and minorities have found the opportunities for them to be limited as well. However, women and minorities are important role models for children who may find that their opportunities are limited by virtue of their race, gender, or socioeconomic status. Children in poor districts must know that there is hope for them to achieve their goals.

In an emergency, Mrs. Cox made a unilateral administrative decision. She had to consider the big picture. It was unfortunate that it was Ms. Thomas and her program that was affected; however, it may have been the most efficient solution at the moment. It is important that Latisha Thomas, from the start, make it known that she wants to be a good citizen of the school. She should make it a point to eat lunch with the other faculty, to attend faculty meetings, volunteer for committees, and assume responsibilities for recess, lunch, and bus duties just like everyone else. As time goes by, if she finds that there are truly issues of bias and discrimination, then there are formal procedures and channels for her to follow. Latisha must not be guilty of that which she is accusing Mrs. Cox. She must not prejudge or second-guess Mrs. Cox's motives before she understands all of the factors. The first week will be difficult, no doubt; however, her cooperation and good spirits throughout the period of inconvenience will pay dividends for her in the end.

In terms of the importance of music in the school, the perception of the music teacher and that the subject has a low priority in the school program, there are many issues to explore. The Music Educators National Conference (MENC) had materials prepared to help teachers and communities with advocacy projects. Many states have formed alliances to promote music education in the schools. In many instances music teachers are fighting negative attitudes adults have toward music in the schools because they remember poor music programs as children themselves. In fact, many of the programs of the past did not produce a generation of adults that value music as an important part of a child's education. They have bad memories of music programs and music teachers. This is unfortunate but true. It is up to you to change that paradigm. Connect the values of school music to the goals of the school, the district, and the community. In the publication *Growing Up Complete*, MENC suggests that music is important because:

1. Music is worth knowing.
2. Music is one of the most important manifestations of our cultural heritage.
3. Music is a potential in every individual that, like all potentials, should be developed to its fullest.
4. Music provides an outlet for creativity, self-expression, and individual uniqueness. It enables us to express our most noble thoughts and feelings.
5. Music teaches students about unique aspects of their relationships with other human beings and with the world around them, in their own and in other cultures.
6. Music opens avenues of success for students who may have problems in other areas of the curriculum and opens approaches to learning that can be applied in other contexts.
7. Music increases the satisfaction students derive from studying music by sharpening sensitivity, raising their level of appreciation, and expanding their musical horizons.
8. Music is one of the most powerful and profound symbol systems that exists.
9. Music helps students learn a significant lesson—that not all aspects of life are quantifiable.
10. Music exalts the human spirit.

(Adapted from The School Music Program: Description and Standards, Music Educators National Conference, second ed., 1987.)

Improvisation

A. Generate a list of musical compositions that could be used in general music lessons that reinforce self-esteem, tolerance, and respect for one another.

or

Generate a list of reasons why music is an essential part of the school curriculum that are not included in *Growing Up Complete*.

B. Write a lesson plan that could be taught in a classroom that is not a music room. What could you do without your resources?

or

Develop a music advocacy project. How can you involve students, parents, and school personnel in a creative way?

Recapitulation

A. Share your lesson plan or advocacy project with your teacher and your classmates for feedback.

B. Peer teach your lesson plans or put your advocacy plan into action.

Mr. Holland, Opus 2

Introduction

A few years ago a film called Mr. *Holland's Opus* told the story of a composer who chose to teach music because he could not make a living as a composer. At first his heart was not in it. His classes were miserable, and consequently he was miserable as well. The old adage, "those who can, do; and those who can't, teach" was certainly true in Mr. Holland's case. It was not until Mr. Holland made the commitment to teaching that his classes turned around.

Perhaps you have faced the same issues. Perhaps you always dreamed of a performing career but chose education as an insurance policy. Certainly, it is important for teachers to be good musicians. A lucky few are able to combine teaching and performing. In the case that follows, Brandon Rockaway faces that dilemma. Is teaching the easy way out?

Exposition

A. Read the Case: Mr. *Holland, Opus 2*
Brandon Rockaway was ready for a teaching career, or at least so he thought. He had many choices upon entering college.

His parents had hoped he would pursue his interest in engineering. His grandfather had dreams of him taking over the family law practice. But Brandon saw his future in music; and the most likely way to make a decent wage in music would be as a teacher.

Brandon wasn't sure how he felt about teaching, but anything that allowed him to actively pursue his artistic goals couldn't be a bad idea. His musicianship was without question. His parents had started him on clarinet when he was barely six years old. By the time he was in the fourth grade, he had picked up the saxophone as well. The sax became his mainstay all the way through high school and into college. Amidst his studies, he somehow always found time for a few freelance gigs: theme parks, Top 40 bands, and even an occasional spot at one of the big jazz clubs in the city. It was here that he found his greatest encouragement from a couple of pros who did a lot of studio work. "Keep up those chops, Brandon! You have a career ahead of you there!"

Occasionally, Brandon's success got in his way. Too many late nights doing freelance work makes for a college student that is distracted at best, exhausted at worst. But Brandon's professors recognized his talent and would give him the necessary leeway to keep up with his work. They all knew of his dreams to one day become a professional studio musician, and in some way, perhaps a bit of extra tolerance and understanding would help.

Graduation came, and Brandon hit the streets in search of his first job. A cruise line offered him a three-month engagement on the Caribbean, or he could do some pick-up jobs that might provide him with enough money to live on, but neither offered the kind of stability he had hoped for. He decided to stay in town for another year and keep studying. This would give him one more year with his teacher who had single-handedly changed his approach to style and tone, while allowing him some time to build up his bank account for the day he decided to go "make it big."

It was a fortunate break that Robinson Middle School, just ten miles away in the neighboring town, was looking for an instrumental teacher. They had an excellent program that even featured a jazz ensemble in addition to two concert bands and a beginning instruments class. Brandon saw this as the perfect opportunity.

Brandon had no trouble getting the job. Other music teachers in the district knew who he was and how hard he was working at his musical endeavors. How exciting it would be for the students to have a teacher who was also working professionally on the side.

On the first day of school, he walked into class and was an immediate hit with the students. He told them a few stories about playing jazz in the clubs. He even found an old sax in the storage locker and rattled off a few licks. The students were impressed and eager to learn from a real "working" musician.

Within a few days, instruments were issued, music had been handed out, and rehearsals were underway. Brandon had forgotten what it was like to be in middle school. The smell of day-old fish sticks from the cafeteria next door, the constant announcements over the public address system, but most of all, the incessant noise in the rehearsal room were almost more than he could stand. "They never stop making noise!" Brandon complained to the orchestra teacher. "They're either talking or playing, but they're never listening!"

The orchestra teacher gave a puzzled look of concern, but attributed the phenomenon mostly to the young teacher growing accustomed to adolescent students. He would get over it sooner or later.

As the days passed, frustrations grew on both the part of the young teacher and the students. The performing groups could scarcely make it through a piece without completely falling apart, and the beginning instruments class was a daily cacophony of students unable to create a single intentional pitch. Mr. Rockaway would try to regain control by picking up his horn and demonstrating with incredible ease, but the students were no longer mesmerized by his talent. They would continue to taunt one another and act out until Mr. Rockaway would finally burst out in a fit of rage. In time, even this had little or no impact on regaining order in the classroom.

As the fall concert approached, word somehow made it to Ms. Jenkins, the kind and experienced Vice Principal who had seen such potential in Brandon Rockaway during his interview. She, herself, had not been a music teacher, but had sung for years in the community choir and had a love and appreciation for music and the musicians that had inspired her over the years. It seemed time that she might pay a visit to Mr. Rockaway's classroom to see if she could be of some help.

As she walked down the hallway during fourth-period band, she could hear nothing but discord and yelling from an ensemble that was supposedly just days away from a concert. She hesitated outside the door for a moment as the instructor got their attention long enough to muster a downbeat. The sound was lackluster and out of tune, wrong notes blaring out that would be obvious to the most untrained of ears. Yet they continued to play, almost as if there were no conductor at all. No sooner had they reached the final chord than the din erupted again, with hardly a chance for the director to address the serious reparations needed.

Ms. Jenkins entered the bandroom and found an empty chair back near the storage lockers. As if on cue, the room fell silent. Brandon Rockaway was stunned.

The students at Robinson had a great deal of love and respect for Eleanor Jenkins. Her work with the student government class was innovative and extraordinary. She had a way of making students motivate themselves with one another, particularly when it came to long-term projects involving community outreach. Many parents remembered her as a teacher at West Park Elementary where she had taught fifth grade for nearly fifteen years before coming to the middle school. There were stories of her strict discipline that were only overshadowed by her extreme exuberance for learning and exploring new concepts and ideas. At Robinson, even students that only knew her from seeing her around campus knew they were in the presence of a great teacher and leader.

"Sorry to interrupt, Mr. Rockaway." Eleanor Jenkins spoke softly with a smile. "You may proceed."

Mr. Rockaway looked out over his class of attentive students for perhaps the first time this year. "Blue Ridge Overture, let's take it from the beginning."

The band raised their instruments and once more started the piece they had muddled through just prior to Ms. Jenkin's arrival. The brass continued to blare, the woodwinds continued to squeak, yet the band played on.

Five minutes and thirty-two seconds later, the band once again reached the final cadence with no more dignity or poise than they had the first time. Mr. Rockaway glanced up at the clock. Four minutes to go until the traditional time to pack up. "Okay, folks, that was pretty good, you can put it away for today."

The clamor erupted again as fifty-eight seventh and eighth graders stampeded through the folding chairs toward the storage lockers behind Ms. Jenkins. "Hi, Ms. Jenkins, why are you here?" could be heard above the roar.

The electronic bell finally released the captive young musicians for lunch as Eleanor Jenkins motioned to Brandon Rockaway who was across the room still trying to dislodge a mouthpiece from a trumpet that had fallen off a chair. "Let's take a walk, Mr. Rockaway."

"They're pretty wild this week. I guess they're excited about the concert." Brandon felt obligated to start the conversation somehow in his defense.

"Yes, they're certainly wound up," agreed Ms. Jenkins. "So . . . do you think they're ready for next Thursday night?"

"Well, at first I thought my standards were too high. I guess things have changed. When I was in school, kids could really play! We did music a lot tougher than we're doing here and most of us couldn't get enough of it." Brandon was rationalizing as he spoke. "But now that I see where they're at, things seem to be going better."

"Really . . . I see." Eleanor Jenkins wasn't buying it.

Uncomfortable with the silence, Brandon continued his testimony. "Why is it that kids have so little interest in learning these days, Ms. Jenkins?"

Ms. Jenkins abruptly changed the subject. "Did you like what you were hearing, Mr. Rockaway?"

"Well, no, but what can you do with a class like this? They don't want to listen to what I have to say. Believe me, I've tried."

"I believe you let them go early today, and they were still ready to work. You might have tried something then."

"I know what you're saying, Ms. Jenkins. But every time I stop the band, they just want to talk, laugh, and fix their hair. It's better if I just keep them playing."

Eleanor Jenkins stopped and turned toward the young music teacher. "Do you have a passion for music, Mr. Rockaway?"

Brandon was stunned. What a ridiculous question. "Of course I do!"

"How about teaching? Do you have a passion for teaching?" The vice principal was driving towards a point.

"Well, sure, I guess, but that's different . . ."

"Is it?" Ms. Jenkins changed her pursuit. "Think back, Mr. Rockaway, to a teacher that really made an impression on you. It doesn't even have to be a music teacher, just someone who made you think."

"Besides my music teachers?" Mr. Rockaway stopped to ponder for a moment. "You know I had a math teacher in tenth grade that really helped turn me around. I wasn't very good in math, but for some reason, he wouldn't give up on me. He was determined that I and everyone else in the class were somehow going to grasp geometry. Pretty soon I was going in at lunchtime and after school on my own will, and I ended up with an A- in the class."

"So what happened there, Brandon?" Ms. Jenkin's tone softened a bit. "Why were you willing to work so hard?"

"I guess it was because the guy cared about me and my success in the class." Brandon relived the experience. "He thought math was really important, and he would talk to us in a way which we could understand. He would never give up."

"You know, Brandon, I've heard you play, and I know what an artist you are, but I would submit to you that as a teacher you must be an artist in two disciplines—that of music and that of teaching." Eleanor Jenkins hesitated before finishing her thought. "Mr. Rockaway, do you really want to be a teacher?"

"Of course." He was defensive. "Music is what I do!"

"No, I didn't say musician." She paused again. "Do you want to be a teacher?"

Brandon stood silent as he reflected over the last eight weeks of chaos in his classroom. He thought back to the teachers who had touched his life and recounted the charisma and dedication that was common to each one of them. "I'm not sure, Ms. Jenkins. To tell you the truth, I'm just not sure."

B. As a class, in groups or in your journal answer the following questions:

1. What's happening (or not happening) in Brandon's classroom? How do the components of rehearsal technique and discipline correspond with one another? What other considerations must you have when you are working with young musicians?
2. What is the nature of Brandon's dilemma? What are the attributes of an effective music teacher? Is it simply enough to be an outstanding musician? Discuss the leading qualities of excellent teachers you have had in the past.

Development

A. Decorate the creature below so that we know he or she is an outstanding music teacher. Share your creations with your classmates along with a few words about what you have drawn. You may wish to duplicate and enlarge the creature before you decorate it.

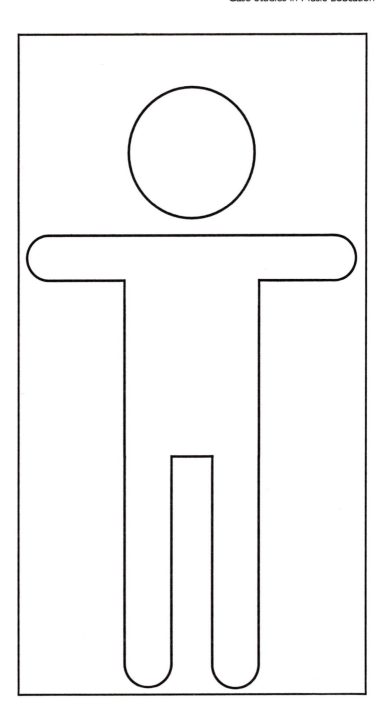

B. Teaching as an Art Form

On the subject of teaching and the understanding of musical ideas, Leonard Bernstein has been quoted as saying, "It was an initiation into the love of learning, of learning how to learn . . . as a matter of interdisciplinary cognition—that is, learning to know something by its relation to something else." This process of "learning how to learn" might only be surpassed by the similar challenge of learning how to teach. Teaching is something that many take for granted, including one young band teacher, Brandon Rockaway. As Bernstein recognized, the essence of learning is the realization of how things relate to one another. Thus, the mark of a successful teacher is to be able to instill the passion and enthusiasm in his or her students that make them want to understand exactly how that occurs. Nearly everyone has encountered at one time or another a music director who lacks passion and the ability to motivate. Likewise, there is no shortage of those teeming with passion and charisma, but who have little to say and are ill-equipped to say it. The true artist is one that is able to engage the imagination of those who learn in a variety of different ways, and help them discover the need within themselves to expand their present understanding of the world around them.

Author and motivational speaker, Tim Lautzenheiser has done extensive study and research on identifying the attributes that create a successful music teacher. In his book *The Art of Successful Teaching*, he tries to identify those elements which we might label as cognitive skills, and those elements that belong to the affective domain which tend to surface as attitudes. The essence of Lautzenheiser's discovery is that assuming one is equipped with the appropriate technical skills, success in the classroom will be a result of the teacher's personal attitude, and similarly the attitudes he or she is able to elicit from the students. Specific components such as compassion, communication, enjoyment, fairness, respect, and a sense of humor all contribute to the total person that is suited for the challenge of teaching music.

While it may seem obvious, the selection of appropriate literature and instructional materials will be the first step toward achieving the success that Lautzenheiser and Bernstein seem to have in mind. "Choose music that you love" are words to live by. If the subject matter does not inspire you, how can you expect anyone else in the room to become even remotely interested? For younger ensembles and general music classes, this may require some time and research on the part of the teacher, but there are increasingly innovative materials on the market that offer editions and classroom materials for nearly any level of ability and that reflect cultural and ethnic diversity as well. The successful teacher will be constantly searching for such literature that is not only of the highest quality, but speaks to himself or herself on a very personal level. Ultimately, the students must sense that you, as the teacher, have something that cannot wait to be shared and experienced. Enthusiasm is contagious, not only in its ability to engage students, but also as a catalyst in keeping things moving, thus lessening classroom management challenges as well.

Lautzenheiser also talks about the process of setting goals and their importance to achieving success. In fact, any motivational speaker will reaffirm the fact that without a sense of where you are going, there is little hope of getting there. The setting of goals has many manifestations: the development of objectives in daily lesson planning, the ideal musical sound that should emerge in the course of rehearsal, and even a long-range vision that holds ambitions which may be unattainable in the present but have the potential of becoming an exciting reality of the future. A survey of people who are thought of as charismatic leaders will reveal that they all have one thing in common: a vision of what might be if they are able to persuade the people around them into following their lead. Consequently, that *which might be* usually becomes that *which is*. Students are willing to go to considerable effort with little immediate reward if they feel that they are part of something much greater than themselves. This doesn't mean that you shouldn't work to create smaller incremental rewards on a daily basis, but it does attest to why some students will stay with a winning team or performing group even when the daily interactions with the person in charge are generally negative and abrasive. Hence, imagine the potential of a teacher who maintains a positive, encouraging attitude on a daily basis, but has a clear design for the future as well.

Joseph Flummerfelt has been preparing choruses for the New York Philharmonic and Philadelphia Orchestra for the past twenty-five years. In regard to the value of music education, he states, "the realization of any great music obliges the performer to go far beyond the sounds on the page in understanding spiritual, emotional, and psychological impulses of the work. Through this pursuit . . . [musicians] are encouraged to communicate with a directness which may be fearsome for the individual alone." The implication here is that the essence of teaching music is greater than the music itself. What we do as music teachers is to help our students understand the impulse that creates musical ideas. How can we help them understand that music is itself a reflection of the society into which it is created? We can learn a great deal about the history and philosophy of the people around us, as well as those who have gone before, simply by taking a moment to examine the impetus of artistic expression. What else does music teach? Are we using every opportunity in the classroom that allows the student to solve problems as every professional musician must do when he or she is first presented with a printed score? Mr. Rockaway's solution was to solve the problems for them. A daily routine requiring little of the students, let alone failing to hold them responsible for any gained knowledge or understanding, quickly grew monotonous for the teacher and the students alike.

Being a musician is a thinking activity of the highest level, yet it is often looked upon as a lesser subject with little importance to a comprehensive education. Perhaps this is because many music teachers over the years have failed to allow their students to think and become actively involved in the problem-solving process. Tim Lautzenheiser prints this simple chart in his book:

I hear—I forget;
I see—I remember;
I do—I understand!

If only those teaching music could remember that their first priority is to help their students understand, many elements of classroom management, discipline, and technique would begin to fall into place. Think about how many times students at any level are overheard saying something like, "Well, the teacher of that class just doesn't care." What does that mean? It probably means that the teacher lacks either the ability or motivation to take the time and energy to truly engage each individual student at a level where they can learn, experience, and eventually comprehend.

With this in mind, there is much to learn from a successful music teacher. Few teachers have the luxury of subject matter that is capable of reaching students on such a personal level. Few teachers have the option of forming classes according to ability and interest as is often afforded to teachers of fine arts. The music teacher has a unique opportunity to motivate students toward accomplishments of extraordinary magnitude, all the while giving them tools that could help them with any subject area that requires analytical and creative abilities. Music can teach a way of thinking, a process of feeling, and can provide an approach for interpreting all skills that will be of vital importance for the rest of one's life. All this, if only the teacher is willing to let real learning take place.

"Do you want to be a teacher, Mr. Rockaway?" seemed to be a simple question for the fledgling band instructor. Ultimately, Mr. Rockaway will have to recognize the difference between the art of music and the art of teaching, and decide whether he is willing and able to let them coalesce in the classroom. His failure to do so will only bring him additional frustration while discouraging students who are earnestly interested in developing their musical skills. Conversely, if he is able to embrace teaching with the same passion that inspires his work at the saxophone, he, too, will touch lives and find success that he couldn't dream possible. Oliver Wendell Holmes once said, "One's mind, once stretched by a new idea, never regains its original dimensions." In this quest, Brandon Rockaway will truly come to know the art of teaching.

Improvisation

A. In small groups, create a list of specific attributes that are commonly found in good teachers. You may wish to make a second list of particular things that take place when an effective teacher is in charge. For example, "Good teachers don't take a lot of time talking about the music, they teach by doing the music."

B. Write a thank-you letter to a teacher who was particularly inspirational in your life. Be sure to mention those specific elements that made them extraordinary and memorable.

or

Write a letter to your professor explaining why you want to be a music teacher. What unique attributes will you bring to the profession?

Recapitulation

A. Having written the above letter, take a moment to identify what you consider to be the singular most important attribute of a successful music teacher.

B. Share your conclusions with the other members of the class.

A Sound Decision

Introduction

Effective music teaching is more than developing lessons around a particular piece of musical literature or theoretical concept. Effective music teaching helps children to form values. Which values we teach is a question that stirs controversy whenever it is asked. However, it is the music teacher's responsibility to make informed decisions regarding what to teach, how to teach, and, in the case of Helen Larson and her headmaster, why to teach. Examining our philosophy of music education provides some insight because philosophy grounds our programs. Often the study of philosophy of music education is reserved for graduate programs. Unfortunately, this may be too late. Music teachers at every stage of their careers make educational decisions each day and in every lesson they write and teach. These decisions are based on their personal philosophy and on the philosophy of the school where they teach. The connections between the individual philosophy and the school philosophy are often political issues. In any case, they must be informed decisions that are taken seriously and discussed by all concerned.

Exposition

A. Consider the issues in the Case: *A Sound Decision*

Helen Larson loved her job. She had been the music teacher at Whitman Preparatory School for three years. In that short time she had built a program of which she was proud. Her children could read musical notation and could speak intelligently about musical issues. Even her kindergarten students could demonstrate the Kodály hand signs and knew a varied repertoire of folk songs.

When Helen arrived at Whitman the program was on the fringe. There were very few resources and the music room, although spacious, looked as if it could be any classroom. Except for a piano and a CD player, there was little evidence that this was the space where music learning was to take place. Over the three years, Helen changed that. She purchased Orff instruments, a new Basal music series, many CDs and music videos, and a set of hand chimes. She organized a fourth- and fifth-grade chorus and an upper school choir. She met with her handbells groups after school and formed a beginning and an advanced Orff ensemble that performed at school concerts. She instituted an upper school musical and brought in a Suzuki violin teacher to begin string instruction in the lower grades.

Helen never lost sight of her goal. She wanted a comprehensive music curriculum which would meet national standards and State core proficiencies. Her goal was to provide students with musical skills that would lead to musical literacy. Her method was eclectic but always with solid musical skills at the foundation.

Helen's objectives for the music program were consistent with the goals of the school. Whitman was an expensive private school in an East Coast college town. Obtaining entrance to prestigious prep schools and later to ivy league universities were the goals of the parents whose children enrolled. Helen was comfortable with the aggressive approach to academics and felt that a strong music program would nurture creative thinking and provide alternatives for children who demonstrated artistic gifts. Parents seemed happy with the program, too. Several had donated money to purchase a new set of risers for the music room and had provided funds for enrichment programs brought into the school.

Dr. Preston Williams, the headmaster, came to Whitman from a private school in New England last year. He was hired because of his successful record of fund-raising and development. At his previous school, he had increased the endowment and enrollment while he supervised the building of a new academic wing. Whitman needed such a leader to prepare the school for the future.

Williams wasted no time making changes at Whitman. He instituted a staff development program and brought in guest speakers from the university. He also began a capital campaign to renovate the physical plant and to build a new upper school classroom building. It was clear that fund-raising was on the top of his agenda at Whitman as it had been in New England.

Preston Williams was also delighted to have found such a valuable resource in Helen, the music teacher. He admired her expertise and seemed pleased with what she had done for the children in the music program at Whitman. In fact, he was eager to work with her and to include her in his plans for Whitman's future.

At the beginning of the school year, Headmaster Williams stopped by the music room at least once a day just to see what was going on. Helen was thrilled to have an administrator take such an active interest in her work. She was extremely proud of her students and their levels of accomplishment in the music classroom.

One afternoon in early October, Williams stopped Helen in the hallway to commend her for her work. Helen humbly acknowledged the praise and stood attentively as the headmaster continued on about his goals for the Whitman School of the future. Suddenly Helen's face turned cold as she realized Williams' agenda and her place in his plans.

"But you know Helen, you may want to revamp your curriculum a bit. I mean, do you think it's really necessary to spend all that time on, how do you say, musical literacy activities?" Clearly, the Headmaster had an agenda.

"Musical literacy activities?" Helen responded, her voice a

bit shaky as she tried to sort out what was happening.

"Well, let's face it, music is fun!" His enthusiasm was somewhere between contagious and frightening. "You make it fun. That's your gift! And you owe it to the children and the school to really capitalize on that." Then he continued, "In five years, who will care if they can read music? What counts is how they touch the parents and grandparents at school programs." He added, "These are potential donors to the school. The children must perform more Helen, don't you think?"

Helen was speechless. "I . . . I'll give this some thought, Dr. Williams."

"Just let them perform, Helen," Williams encouraged. "I guarantee, we'll all come out ahead in the end."

For the entire year, Helen did just that. She used her general music classroom time to prepare the children to perform. They sang at programs for Thanksgiving, Grandparent's Day, Founder's Day and Mother's Day. The children performed at a holiday concert and a spring concert. After each performance Helen received congratulatory notes from members of the Board of Trustees, parents, and teachers. Everyone seemed happy. Everyone except Helen, that is.

Headmaster Williams was especially pleased. He, too, had written Helen and her students notes of congratulations and praise. In fact, when she appeared in his office for her annual review, he said, "Helen, you've done a wonderful job, and everyone loves your kids! I'm sure you agree that our decision to focus on performance was a sound choice. We all think you are amazing! I am recommending to the Board of Trustees that you receive a substantial raise for next year."

Helen smiled and thanked him, but she also felt uneasy. Although she recognized the value of musical performance, she advocated a program that had more balance. She was firmly committed to the development of musical skills. She knew in her heart that the curriculum had not met her own standards, and she felt that her children were somehow cheated.

Now what? On the one hand, Helen was pleased to receive such a glowing evaluation, and she could certainly use the additional money. However, on the other hand, she believed a program that is solely based on performance undermined quality music education.

B. Discuss Helen's dilemma. What should she do? How can she make everyone happy? What are her options?

Development

A. Watch an hour of music television on one of the cable channels. Think about how this music reflects our society. For instance, has musical performance become as much a visual experience as it is an aural one? What values can be gleaned from the music on TV? What can we learn about youth from watching and listening to their music?

B. The focus of what we teach, the values we impart, and our point of view are reflective of our philosophy of music education. As practitioners, teachers sometimes forget the importance of thinking about philosophy. With many classes to teach, lesson plans to write, ensembles to rehearse along with bus, lunchroom, and recess duties, teachers feel they are lucky if they merely "survive." Many find refuge in the Basal music series or in materials collected from in-service workshops. Teachers trained or certified in one of the major music teaching methods feel that their curriculum is preset. It is not surprising that many music teachers fall victim to the "store-bought" materials readily available.

Thinking about philosophy is important. What should music education do for the children you teach? Should musical literacy be the goal of a musical education? Should the nurturing of audiences be the focus? Should performance be the driving force? How will the experiences in your music classes contribute to the goals of the school, the school district, and national educational agendas? For example, there is much concern at the federal level that Americans be first in business, mathematics, and science. Can your music program contribute to this goal? Many educators feel that children need to be thinking critically. Can you do critical thinking in a music program? What kinds of critical thinking can a kindergarten child do in music?

If we have done anything well in school music programs in the last fifty years, it has been in the development of ensembles. Everyone knows of that award-winning school band, orchestra, or choir. We have been able to take large numbers of students varying in levels of potential and ability and train them to perform at very high levels. We have been successful in convincing school administrators that our ensembles should be included within the school day and that students in ensembles should be graded as they would in any other school subject. In many high schools, the ensembles are the music program. Finally, we have made schools and their communities very proud of the accomplishments of the members of school ensembles.

What we have not done well is to instill in the general public the importance of music throughout life. Those same individuals who as children played in award-winning school ensembles have become adults who are eliminating school music programs. Somehow, we did not make the essential connections to music as an art form, as a lens through which one learns to see and appreciate that which is beautiful. While the contemporary musical culture thrives, symphony orchestras scramble to fill seats in their concert halls and have resorted to advertising that appeals to the lowest common denominator. One radio ad for a world renowned orchestra began, "Even if you thought Schubert was a dessert," and ended with a plea that, "You don't have to know anything about music to subscribe to and enjoy the. . . orchestra." This tells a great deal about our success as music educators over the years. Even Mr. Holland and his former clarinet student who became state governor could not deter the music program cuts in the school budget.

The future of school music programs depends upon how successfully we can tie our goals as music educators to the global goals of the schools. In Helen Lawson's case, the goals of the school are clear. Parents want aggressive academics. They want their children to be critical thinkers. In other situations the goals may be different. Some schools see their mission as developing citizens for a democratic society. As the minority population in some districts becomes the majority, schools have placed multicultural issues at the forefront. As everyone fights for the dollar, it is those programs, which contribute to the mission of the school, that survive. Our job as music educators and school teachers is to show the public how we do it.

For nearly a generation, music educators have aligned music education with aesthetic education. Cultivating the aesthetic experience has been paramount in the minds of educators who feel that the results of music education should enable students to make value judgments, recognize the beauty in good music as art, and come to appreciate musical expression as a form of connoisseurship. Since all human beings have a potential for music, it is the responsibility of school programs to teach children to find satisfaction and meaning through experiencing it. For a long time, music was in schools to provide a worthwhile use of leisure time. By studying about music, children became informed listeners and consumers. They were the ones, we thought, who would buy classical CDs and purchase subscriptions to the symphony orchestra. They were also the ones who would join the community and church choirs, sing to their children when they were young, and be life-long "lovers" of the art form. For them this would provide a better quality of life. In his philosophy of music education, Bennett Reimer, in his book, A *Philosophy of Music Education*, writes, "Music is a way to know the world [and] to create and share meaning in the world" (p. 77). "The primary function of aesthetic education," he says, "is to help people share the meanings which come from expressive forms" (p. 95). He continues, "the experience of music as expressive form is the be-all and end-all of music education, for such experience is the only way of sharing music's aesthetic meaning" (p. 96).

This view has been challenged by philosophers who believe that music is a form and a source of knowledge that can best be acquired through performance. This view of children as "musicers" engaged in the act of "musicing" is called a praxial philosophy because it applies theory in practice. Advocates of this philosophy such as David Elliott and Doreen Rao believe that musical performance is the essence of music education.

Howard Gardner theorizes that music is a form of intelligence. It is one of many aptitudes which all humans possess. Gardner believes that the heart of any arts-educational process (such as music education) must be the development of the child's capacity to think musically. Therefore, music education should provide children with opportunities where they can think in the medium of music. This view holds that the performance of music, then, is the cornerstone of a curriculum that focuses on making music through performance, developing skills of perception, and asking students to be reflective and critical throughout the process. This will work for Helen because it is a notion that is consistent with the mission at Whitman.

The future of school music programs depends upon how successfully we can tie our goals as music educators to the global goals of the schools. In Helen's situation, she must realize that private schools are enrollment driven. They compete for dollars in order to exist. If outstanding musical ensembles and quality musical performances attract an audience of potential donors, then so be it. Helen must look broadly at the variety of philosophies of music education to find one that will support the school's agenda and her own personal goals. Remember the following words of caution: methodologies may be eclectic. Teaching approaches may be combined. Musical literature and classroom materials may be selected from varied sources. However, philosophy must be singular. For Helen, at Whitman the issue of what to teach is not as important as why. She must decide for herself what the purpose of her program should be and then articulate that clearly to the headmaster. Perhaps teaching musical skills in the general music classroom will enhance the performance of the ensembles. Then the curriculum will fall into place. An eclectic philosophy that takes a bit from here and a bit from there will not yield the kind of music programs our schools need.

Improvisation

A. Read each of the following philosophical quotes. Place a star next to the one you find the most meaningful. Discuss with your classmates.

G Music education must make the development of procedural musical knowledge [skills] meaningful by enabling and permitting students to generate and evaluate musical performances that are personally meaningful and sequentially developmental. When a student's procedural knowledge is carefully challenged with musical opportunities of appropriate complexity, he/she is likely to achieve the enjoyment or intrinsic reward that comes with doing something that is worth doing for its own sake.

—paraphrase of Mihalyi Csikszentmihalyi

•

R Music has unique qualities that make it the most desirable medium of organized aesthetic education. Human beings are universally responsive to music and can find satisfaction and meaning through experience with it.

—Charles Leonhard and Robert W. House

•

R Children "must be given the opportunity to develop their aesthetic potentials to the highest possible levels through expressive experience with music of the highest possible quality." This extensive experience with music, they posit, will yield in children extrinsic values that will be "resources for enriched home and community life, and the opportunity to discover unusual talent."

—Charles Leonhard and Robert W. House

•

Music is a way to know the world [and] to create and share meaning in the world.

—Bennett Reimer

•

In music, a person who is able to 1) notice the common features of the sounds of Beethoven's music, 2) give the proper name to that noticing ("that's Beethoven"), and 3) do so regularly whenever a piece of Beethoven is played can be assumed to have the concept of "Beethoven-ness."

—Bennett Reimer

•

[Musical performance is a means that allows students to] reconstruct the steps and understand the rationales behind the steps a composer/performer took to compose/perform a piece, then students will come to a conceptual understanding of the piece. This allows students to gain a sense of the intelligence involved in the construction of the product: a sense of musical decision-making processes, of strategies available within a specific musical style, of the problems that a composer and/or performer had to face in producing the musical product, and perhaps a sense of the motivations underlying the composing and/or performing process as a whole. It provides a basis for understanding similar works or aspects of dissimilar works. Performing breathes life into what might otherwise be studied and misunderstood as a collection of precious but distant objects. It alters one's perspective on musical products. Once performed, music is listened to not as mere objects, and not just with the ears, but with the whole self.

—David Elliott and Doreen Rao

Among the Veda people . . . the belief is that everyone has the ability to perform and make sense of music. The only reason some are better than others is that they are more committed or they work harder.

—Elizabeth Oehrle

•

In Africa "exposure to musical situations and participation are emphasized more than formal training. The basic principle is that of learning through social experience." The organization of traditional music in social life enables people to acquire their musical knowledge in slow steps from an early age. They learn aurally and orally moving from simple to complex musical ideas as they engage in music-making.

—Elizabeth Oehrle

•

In their arts, Africans are directly involved in bringing quality to a social situation.

—Elizabeth Oehrle

B. Make a list of the global goals of general education. Look in the newspapers and professional journals for ideas. Contact a nearby school district office for a copy of the goals and objectives for that school system. Then create your own philosophy for a school music program. How does it support the global goals of general education? Write it out and then design a visual "logo" depicting your philosophy's main themes.

Recapitulation

A. Share ideas with your classmates or colleagues.

B. Role-play a meeting with Dr. Williams to present your case.

Playing for Pleasure

Introduction

In this case, the student, her family, and her teacher are faced with a dilemma. The school program has requirements and procedures that place all of the actors in an uncomfortable position. The teacher must decide how far she is willing to bend the rules and fight the administration on behalf of the needs of her students. Although the teacher in this case is an applied piano teacher, the issue she faces is one that is appropriate to teachers in classrooms and ensemble situations as well.

Exposition

A. Read the Case: *Playing for Pleasure*
Leila Wilkinson had been teaching for ten years at the local community music school. As a conscientious teacher, she took pride in the accomplishments of her students. She was pleased when they entered competitions and won awards. She encouraged them to play new repertoire, to seek out personal interpretations of the standards and classics, and to attend concerts and hear great pianists when they came to town. She was a very popular teacher. Her students loved her. The administration

of the music school also loved her. Leila followed the rules. She knew the policies of the school and followed procedures to the letter.

Emily was eleven years old when she asked her parents for piano lessons. There had always been a piano in her home and Emily had attended youth concerts at the symphony since she was small. Emily's parents wanted her to enjoy the piano; therefore, they proceeded very cautiously. At school, Emily was having a difficult time. She was withdrawn, unhappy, and showed little motivation. Since she thought her teacher did not like her, she did not like school. Emily's parents wanted her to have quality instruction from a teacher who taught children, rather than from a teacher who taught piano.

Leila Wilkinson seemed to fit the bill. In addition to being an accomplished performer and composer, her reputation as a piano teacher was well-known. Emily began lessons and things seemed to be going well. She was encouraged to compose music for her lessons and her teacher even wrote a few etudes especially for her. Before her parents arrived home from work, Emily practiced each day when she came home from school. In fact, they never really heard her practice; however, her older brother was home each afternoon with her and corroborated her claims to be practicing. The piano teacher seemed pleased and reported that Emily was making steady progress. And Emily seemed to love her teacher. She insisted that the entire family attend a recital of original compositions played by her teacher at the college.

Emily's school work began to improve as well. Her teacher noticed that Emily seemed happier. Emily joined the student council and the sixth grade choir. In class, Emily began to participate in discussion. She also started playing with a large group of new friends during recess.

It was May when things began to fall apart. For some reason unknown to her parents, Emily began to lose interest in playing the piano. Her brother reported that she had stopped practicing. On lesson days she would complain of an upset stomach or a headache, or of having too much homework. She clearly did not want to go to her piano lesson. Something was not right.

Emily's teacher began to complain as well. Emily was not prepared for her lessons, and she was not meeting her expectations. Finally, there was a family meeting at Emily's house. "What's wrong?" Emily's mother asked. "I thought you loved your lessons and your teacher."

"I do," replied Emily. "It's just that my teacher is forcing me to play in her end of the year studio recital. Mom, I don't want to do it. I don't want to play in public." Emily started to cry. It seemed that Emily just wanted to play for pleasure. "Playing the piano is for me, and me alone," Emily sobbed. "I don't see why I have to play for or in front of anyone else."

Emily's mother did not know how to react. "Are all the students required to play in the recital?" she asked.

"Yes," replied Emily.

That evening Emily's mother called the piano teacher. Emily's story was correct. Each year, students present a public recital. It was a requirement of the college preparatory program. In a sense it was similar to the jury exams college students take when they major in performance. No one ever really likes doing them, it is just a fact of life. Her teacher further explained that the director of the preparatory school attended the studio recitals to evaluate each teacher's effectiveness. Those evaluations were used to determine whether teachers were rehired or received salary raises. If Emily did not play in the recital, it might jeopardize her teacher's job. It was a real dilemma.

B. As a class, in groups or in your personal journal, address the following:

What are the issues here? Is Emily justified in not wanting to play in the recital? What are the options for Emily's teacher? What should Emily's mother do? Discuss these questions in small groups, then report your conclusions to the class.

Development

A. Divide a piece of drawing paper in half. On the left side, create a logo for a school that is procedural, structured, and bureaucratic. On the right side, create a logo for a school that is caring, concerned, and connected to students as individuals. Share your logos with your classmates. Then, choose a piece of music that represents the bureaucratic model and another that represents a child-centered approach. Explain and defend your choices to the class.

B. There are many ways that schools are organized. A common one is the bureaucratic model. Bureaucratic schools thrive on rules and procedures. Principals believe that when there is a strong structure in place, buildings run efficiently. Teachers and students know what is expected. There is a chain of command. From the students to the principal, each person knows their role.

The bureaucratic model became popular during the industrial revolution when schools were expected to prepare students to work in factories. This is the time when desks were aligned in straight rows and often nailed to the floor. The school day was organized into periods of time with a bell sounding, like in the factory, to indicate the beginning and end of the work day, recess, and lunch. In the high school and junior high school, a bell rang to indicate the beginning and end of each class period.

Teachers in bureaucratic schools kept records. They made seating charts and wrote structured lesson plans. Learning experiences were centered on meeting behaviorist objectives that stated what the desired student learning outcome would be for each lesson. Teachers, as specialists in their particular subject, taught the content of their curriculum. Everyone, like each worker in a factory, was treated the same.

A contrasting model describes schools as learning communities that are caring, concerned, and connected. This view, sometimes called the "feminist" perspective, has become popular in the last twenty years as a reaction to schools dominated by male administrators. The old notion that "women teach, while men administrate" has changed and so has the model in which schools are organized. These buildings are student-centered. Teachers teach children the contents of the curriculum. Instruction is individualized as much as possible so that children have the maximum opportunity to meet their unique and different potentials. Some elementary schools are non-graded. This means that a child is not assigned to the first grade or the second grade; rather, children are given learning activities to meet their individual levels. Some buildings have eliminated bells. Other buildings are organized into teams where the teachers meet together to organize learning time and share ideas.

Teaching to individual differences is challenging. In the private studio it is perhaps easier; in the music classroom with many children, it is very difficult. Nevertheless, it is important to take individual differences into account. One music educator who advocates teaching to individual differences is Edwin Gordon. Gordon believes that in order for effective music teaching to take place, teachers must know what the musical potential is for each student. To do that, Gordon suggests that teachers administer a musical aptitude test to each child. These tests identify the musical potential for each student. Once teachers know the test scores, they are able to design teaching materials that enable children to succeed because they are appropriate for their level of learning. Children grow musically when they are presented with materials that are appropriate to their stage of musical development.

In addition to musical aptitude, teachers need to assess the learning styles of their students. This can be done with a test instrument or by understanding the characteristics of the various learning types. The accompanying chart describes four learning types that Bernice McCarthy labels as Type One—Imaginative Learner; Type Two—Analytic Learner; Type Three—Common Sense Learner; and Type Four—Dynamic Learner.

Emily has a high musical aptitude. Her composite scores on Gordon's *Intermediate Measures of Music Audiation* show her to be above average in tonal and rhythm descriptors. The McCarthy

4MAT® STYLE DESCRIPTORS

Type One: *Imaginative Learners*

As students they:
- Learn by listening and sharing ideas
- Are interested in people and culture
- Believe in their own experience
- Rely on their feelings
- Enjoy group discussions that nurture conversation

In music classes they:
- Are first to join the circle
- Enjoy playing classroom instruments
- Sing the loudest
- Will Always volunteer

As teachers they:
- Desire to facilitate individual growth
- Help students become more self aware
- Like discussions and group work
- See knowledge as enhancing personal insight

Type Three: *Common Sense Learners*

As students they:
- Learn by testing theories and ideas
- Need to know how things work
- Enjoy solving problems
- Want learning to be useful in real life
- Like "hands-on" experience

In music classes they:
- Are first to "try it out"
- Are playing when should be listening
- Enjoy worksheets and practice
- Enjoy movement and participatory activities

As teachers they:
- Value productivity and competence
- Give students skills they will need in life
- Encourage practical applications
- Use measured rewards

Type Two: *Analytic Learners*

As students they:
- Learn by thinking through ideas
- Critique information and gather data
- Enjoy traditional classrooms
- Participate by watching
- Enjoy working alone

In music classes they:
- Love the series books
- Like research projects
- Like studying "about" music
- Seldom volunteer for the solo

As teachers they:
- Are interested in transmitting knowledge
- Strive for accuracy
- Teach from a lesson plan and require notebooks
- Like facts, details and organization

Type Four: *Dynamic Learners*

As students they:
- Learn by trial and error
- Tend to take risks
- Need to do it their own way
- Love surprises and relish change
- Reach accurate conclusions without logic

In music classes they:
- Like new things
- Love composing and improvising
- Try things for themselves
- Love to perform for others

As teachers they:
- Are interested in student "self-discovery"
- Encourage experimental learning
- Like variety in instructional methods
- Gear lessons to students' interests

From the 4MAT System: *Teaching To Learning Styles with Right/Left Mode Techniques,* by Bernice McCarthy, copyright 1980, 1987 by Excel, Inc. and *About Learning,* by Bernice McCarthy, copyright 1996 by Excel, Inc. Used by special permission. Not to be further reproduced without the express written permission of Excel, Inc. Those desiring a copy of the complete work for further may acquire it from the publisher, Excel, Inc., 23385 Old Barrington Road, Barrington, IL 60010, 1-800-822-4MAT or 1-847-382-7272, website http://www.excelcorp.com.

Learning Type Measure (LTM) and *Hemispheric Mode Indicator (HMI)* reveal that Emily is a watcher more than a doer. That may explain why she doesn't want to play in public. While she enjoys practicing and studying, Emily is not excited about performance. Teachers of performing ensembles often report having students who come to all of the rehearsals but do not appear for the performance. Like Emily, they enjoy the rehearsals but do not like to perform for an audience. In general music classes, these children also prefer to watch. They are the children that do not always sing, rarely volunteer, and do not like to sing solos. The danger is that teachers, who do not understand learning styles and the limits of musical aptitude, accuse these children of not being interested. Sometimes, they lower the grades of these children in order to punish them for not actively demonstrating participation. As teachers learn to recognize the characteristics of individual learning types, they can more readily adapt instruction appropriately.

There is one word of caution. Understanding and teaching to individual differences is not the same as labeling. Children need to be encouraged to develop their own style, but they must also learn how to be successful in all kinds of musical and classroom situations. Clearly all children can learn. Some may need a bit more time. Although a teacher might be sympathetic to a particular child's learning style or musical aptitude, it is never an excuse for not meeting the standards or expectations of the learning experience. That kind of tracking is not sound educational practice, nor is it ethical.

Improvisation

A. In small groups brainstorm ways that an applied music lesson (such as a piano lesson), a general music class, and a performing ensemble might offer opportunities for children with different learning needs. What kind of musical activities would not lend themselves to lessons, classes, or ensembles?

B. Think about your own learning type. By using the chart on page 66 try to project which category you fit best. Discuss these characteristics with your classmates. Think about your roommate or a significant other. What is his or her learning type? Investigate music aptitude tests. Read the test manuals. What insights do they reveal?

Interview a public school music teacher to find out what accommodations teachers make for children with individual learning needs. Contact an applied music teacher and ask the same questions.

Recapitulation

A. Discuss your findings with your classmates.

B. Assume you are Emily's piano teacher. Write a personal statement to the school director defending your decision to excuse her from the spring recital.

A Perfect Authentic Mess

Introduction

Linda Clarkson believed that if she was prepared and knew her subject matter, all would be golden. She felt that her responsibility was to teach, and it was the students' responsibility to learn. This was the perfect partnership. If students did not learn, Ms. Clarkson blamed their lack of motivation, lack of support at home or peer pressure, which pushed the idea that music was not "cool." It never occurred to her that she was responsible for the learning as well. It makes sense, though, that students do learn when their learning needs are met.

However, Linda's dilemma, she thought, centered on her fundamental belief that music should speak for itself. She believed that music should be taught for its own sake and that activities designed to entertain somehow denigrated music to something lower than it was. "Music for its own sake" was her motto. If she changed her approach, was she selling out?

Exposition

A. Consider the situation described in the Case: A *Perfect Authentic Mess*

69

Linda Clarkson was a music education major with a composition concentration in college. She loved music theory, solfège, and dictation, and worked like a whiz on the computer. She could navigate the MIDI keyboard, synthesizers, and the complex notational programs with ease. She envisioned her ideal job as one where she could teach theory in high school to students who, like her, enjoyed the rules, the analysis, and the challenge of decoding the musical masterpieces of the great composers. Linda also liked contemporary music. Her own compositions were minimalist in genre. And, in a small and modest way, she was one of the disciples of Philip Glass, Steve Reich, and the twentieth-century avant garde.

Linda taught in a small school where the middle school and high school shared the same building. Although her job involved several general music classes for the middle school students, she did have two sections of music theory classes at the high school for students who were interested in chord progressions, harmonic resolutions, sonata form, and the challenge of decoding a melody from dictation. Or so it seemed.

This year had not gone well for Linda. Her general music classes seemed okay, but the music theory course was not successful. Instead of getting students who wanted to study the great masters, she found herself with a class of "rockers"—boys and girls who wanted to arrange commercial music for their own bands, listen to rap in class, and basically "veg out." In fact, many of them did not have the background or skill to accomplish even those goals. Early in the semester, she decided that her students had to have the "basics" before anything could be accomplished. She ordered some theory workbooks and decided to teach them the kind of introduction to music theory and musicianship that she had as a first-year student in college.

As the semester progressed the students became disengaged, and some even became disruptive. Several dropped the course early on, much to the dismay of the vice principal and the guidance department. As the students became more troublesome, Linda's attitude also changed. She no longer looked forward to the music theory class. Instead, she just wanted to get through it each day. In desperation she began to give students large quantities of workbook assignments to do in class, just to keep them quiet.

Margaret Dickson, Linda's supervisor, became very concerned. She knew Linda had great potential and feared that the enthusiasm Linda had when she began teaching would turn into burn-out very quickly. One morning in early February, Dr. Dickson observed a music theory lesson taught from the following plan:

Objectives:
- expose class to good music that they may not get elsewhere
- analyze real music instead of worksheets
- learn to change meter when doing rhythm exercises

Materials:
- recording of the Brahms *Requiem*
- copies of the first page of the fourth movement
- rhythm worksheets

Procedure:
- collect homework
- distribute musical excerpt from the fourth movement of the Brahms *Requiem*
- give class a brief history of Brahms and of his setting of the *Requiem*
- tell class about the recording
- identify the soloists, orchestra, and choir
- play the recording of the fourth movement
- ask the class to listen for overall form, key, and meter
- analyze the first page of the score for the fourth movement and write in the Roman numerals
- ask the class, "Does Brahms bend any of the part-writing rules we have studied?"
- distribute rhythm worksheets, and ask the class about the different meters
- divide the class into small groups and assign each group a

different rhythm while allowing students a brief amount of practice time

- reconvene the class and perform the rhythms for each other
- give a pop quiz
- if time permits, answer any questions about the homework

Dr. Dickson knew that Linda had worked hard on the plan; but it was clear that the plan was not working. In the first place, there was little higher order thinking evident in the content. Although the lesson included an excerpt from the Brahms *Requiem*, it seemed to not have relevance to the students. In the post-observation conference, Dr. Dickson reminded Linda of an in-service program all teachers attended before the opening of the school year. The program consisted of a workshop on learning styles and integrating activities into each lesson that addressed the diversity of learning styles among students. Dr. Dickson wondered if Linda's problem was that her teaching style did not address the learning needs of her students. She offered Linda a model for music lessons that included right brain and left brain teaching strategies and that would engage the students in problem-solving from a holistic perspective. Together they reworked Linda's lesson:

AUTHOR: Margaret Dickson
THEME: Music Communicates a Message
GRADE LEVEL: High School Music Theory

1.	EXPERIENCE
1. OBJECTIVE:	Using visualization and guided imagery, have students generate ideas relative to beauty and emotion.
ACTIVITY:	Using guided imagery have students close their eyes and imagine the most beautiful place they have ever been. Where was it? What was it? Write a brief paragraph describing it.
ASSESSMENT:	Observation of student engagement and excitement.
2. OBJECTIVE:	To engage the students in reflective thinking by listening, interacting, and honoring subjectivity.
ACTIVITY:	Have students in the class share their thoughts by reading the paragraphs to each other.
ASSESSMENT:	Willingness to take a risk by sharing reflections with others; analysis of paragraph; fluency and flexibility of ideas.
2.	**PRESENT**
3. OBJECTIVE	To have the students see relationships and conceptualize.
ACTIVITY:	Have the students select a CD from their personal audio collections that evokes the same feeling and reminds them of that special place. If practical, have the students bring the CD's to class. Play some of the examples as students explain their choices.
ASSESSMENT:	Students show the ability to link ideas through metaphors and symbols.
4. OBJECTIVE:	To present concrete content and develop idea coherence.
ACTIVITY:	Present a lecture on Brahms. Give dates, style, information on, romanticism, expression of emotion, and state why Brahms is important. Include information about *Requiem*. Have the students create a checklist including all of the descriptors that were common in the pieces selected from their personal audio collections.
ASSESSMENT:	Students demonstrate theoretical understanding.

3.	PRACTICE
5. OBJECTIVE:	To practice previously learned information. Students collect data and make decisions.
ACTIVITY:	Read the text of the Brahms Requiem Movt. 4–"How Lovely is They Dwelling Place." Have students listen to the recording and follow the score. What is the key, meter, and form? Does Brahms meet the criteria developed in Step 4? If the answer is "no," ask the students to suggest ways Brahms could change his work to meet the criteria.
ASSESSMENT:	Teacher assesses the student's ability to think logically, analyze data, predict, and form hypotheses. Teacher evaluates choice parameters, accuracy, and thoroughness.
6. OBJECTIVE:	To personalize the information and connect to the concept.
ACTIVITY:	Have students analyze the opening chords using traditional figuration. Present the following problem: If you were going to write a piece describing your favorite place, what might it sound like? In cooperative learning groups find a rhythm that you would use and notate it.
ASSESSMENT:	Teacher assesses student's ability to think logically, analyze data, predict, and form hypotheses. Examine the student's ability to work collaboratively in a group.
4.	EXTEND
7. OBJECTIVE:	To have students revise, edit, and synthesize.
ACTIVITY:	Perform the rhythm for each other.
ASSESSMENT:	Teacher assesses the quality of each student's exhibition.
8. OBJECTIVE:	To exhibit creative work.
Activity:	Listen to Brahms once more. Students describe in their journals the new insights they have gained. Share with the class.
ASSESSMENT:	Teacher assesses the demonstration of the ability to extend concepts and ask new questions.

For homework choose one of the following:

• Design a t-shirt to be sold with the Brahms *Requiem* recording

• You are a writer for *Rolling Stone* magazine assigned to interview Brahams after the premier of his Requiem. What questions would you ask him? Write at least five.

• Listen to Paul McCartney's Liverpool Oratorio. How is its message different from Brahams? Discuss in a well-developed essay.

• Read some poetry by poets living in the Romantic era. Describe how the poems are like music.

B. In small groups discuss the differences between Linda's lesson and the lesson she wrote with her supervisor Dr. Dickson. Notice the correlation to the National Standards (figure A), the higher order thinking (HOT) skills (figure B), and the opportunities for curriculum integration (figure C).

Figure A
Correlation to National Standards

• **STEP 3**
  Content Standard 6: Listening to, analyzing, and describing music
  Content Standard 7: Evaluating music and music performances
  Content Standard 9: Understanding music in relation to
  history and culture

• **STEP 4**
  Content Standard 8: Understanding relationships between music,
  other arts, and disciplines outside the arts
  Content Standard 9: Understanding music in relation to
  history and culture
  Content Standard 6: Listening to, analyzing, and describing music

• **STEP 5**
  Content Standard 5: Reading and notating music
  Content Standard 6: Listening to, analyzing, and describing music
  Content Standard 7: Evaluating music and music performances

• **STEP 6**
  Content Standard 3: Improvising melodies, variations, and
  accompaniment
  Content Standard 4: Composing and arranging music within
  specified guidelines

Content Standard 5: Reading and notating music
Content Standard 6: Listening to, analyzing, and describing music

- **STEP 7**
  Content Standard 7: Evaluating music and music performances

- **STEP 8**
  Content Standard 6: Listening to, analyzing, and describing music

- **HOMEWORK**
  Content Standard 8: Understanding relationships between music, other arts, and disciplines.
  Content Standard 9: Understanding music in relation to history and culture

---

Figure B
Thinking Skills
(Higher order thinking skills are in **boldface**)

Step 1	5.0	Synthesis				
Step 2	2.0	Comprehension	6.0	Evaluation		
Step 3	3.0	Application	4.0	Analysis	5.0	Synthesis
Step 4	1.0	Knowledge	2.0	Comprehension	3.0	Application
Step 5	**4.0**	**Analysis**	**5.0**	**Synthesis**	**6.0**	**Evaluation**
Step 6	3.0	Application	**4.0**	**Analysis**	**5.0**	**Synthesis**
Step 7	3.0	Application	**4.0**	**Analysis**	**6.0**	**Evaluation**
Step 8	3.0	Application	**4.0**	**Analysis**	**5.0**	**Synthesis**
	6.0	**Evaluation**				
Homework	2.0	Comprehension	**4.0**	**Analysis**	**5.0**	**Synthesis**

The thinking skills described above refer to Bloom's Taxonomy as described in his book, *Taxonomy of Objectives in the Cognitive Domain*. Knowlege (1.0), Comprehension (2.0) and Application (3.0) are the lower order thinking skills. **Analyis (4.0), Synthesis (5.0)** and **Evaluation (6.0)** are the higher order thinking skills, referred to in this text as the **HOT** skills.

Figure C
Integrated Curriculum

Step 1	English
Step 4	Social Studies
Step 5	Science (experimentation using the Scientific Method)
	Mathematics–manipulating data
Step 6	Mathematics–manipulating data
Homework	Visual Art, English

Development

A. Examine the following criteria. Notice how Dr. Dickson's lesson meets the criteria.

Criteria for a Successful Lesson

1. The lesson is centered around a musical concept(s) which engages problem-solving.
   Steps 1, 3, 6, 7, and homework
2. The teacher combines strategies which engage the right brain as well as the left.
   Left Brain—Steps 2, 4, 5, 7, and homework
   Right Brain—Steps 1, 3, 6, 8, and homework
3. There is music or music making in the lesson.
   Steps 3, 5, 6, 7, and 8
4. There are strategies which address the diversity of learning types.

Imaginative learner	*Steps 1, 2*
Analytic learner	*Steps 3, 4*
Common Sense learner	*Steps 5, 6*
Dynamic learner	*Steps 7, 8*

   The homework assignment includes one activity for each type of learner.

---

5. Children are asked probing questions which motivate higher order thinking and that involve children in using musical thinking to solve the problem.

Steps 1, 2, 3, 5, 6, 7, 8, and homework

6. The lesson includes musical activities and tasks are authentic.

Steps 3, 4, 5, 6, 7, and 8

7. The teacher checks for understanding at multiple points within the lesson using a variety of evaluative tools. Assessment strategies are included for each step.

Steps 1, 2, 3, 4, 5, 6, 7, and 8

8. The activities provided in the lesson present the evidence students need to solve the problem and provide the preparation for the next music learning experience.

Step 4

9. Musical skills, including but not limited to "auditation," are developed.

Steps 5, 6, and 7

10. The lesson content is aesthetically sound.

Steps 3, 4, 5, 6, 7, and 8

B. A 4MAT for Lesson Planning

In 1972, Bernice McCarthy developed a planning model to help teachers organize their teaching based on differences in the way people learn. Designed to raise teacher awareness as to why some things work with some learners while others do not, her materials synthesized research from the fields of education, psychology, neurology, and management. The theories of David Kolb (1981, 1984, 1985), Carl Jung (1923), Jean Piaget (1970), John Dewey (1958), Joseph Bogen (1969, 1975), Gabriele Rico (1983), Betty Edwards (1979), and John Bradshaw and Norman Nettleton (1983) have contributed to the continued development of McCarthy's concepts.

McCarthy identifies four learning types: imaginative, analytical, common-sense, and dynamic. She bases learning style upon both the perception and the processing of information. Each individual reaches a different balance between these two factors but falls within a certain range that defines his or her learning type.

Type One students are imaginative learners. In combining their tendencies toward concrete experience and reflective observation, these students listen to and share ideas because they believe in their own experiences. They like to make a personal connection with the teacher. In music classes, they are the first to join the circle or play a classroom instrument, and they can be counted on to sing the loudest.

Type Two learners prefer to think about ideas. These analyzers, who favor reflective observation and abstract conceptualization, love working out of basic texts, doing research projects, and studying about music. They tend to watch as their classmates engage in a musical activity rather than participate directly because they like to learn by themselves. These students do not enjoy cooperative learning strategies, and they seldom volunteer to sing or play a solo or to participate in classroom activities.

Type Three students, who combine abstract conceptualization with active experimentation, are the common-sense learners. These children like to solve puzzles and find solutions to problems. They experiment and tinker to discover how things work. These are the children who are likely to take apart their musical instrument and who need to "try things out." They can usually be found playing when they should be listening.

Type Four learners thrive on change and on finding an original way to complete a task. These dynamic learners, who combine active experimentation with their own concrete experiences, are the first to come up with an interesting improvisation or an original composition. Although these students often arrive at the correct answer to a question, they are not likely to use logic in the process; rather they rely on a more intuitive process that is based on both analysis and experience (Abrahams, 1992).

While traditional academic classes generally honor the Type

Two and Type Three learners, music classes and participation in ensembles offer opportunities to address all learning types and to engage students in high level thinking, problem-solving, and the creation of musical excellence. In the university setting, professors more typically focus on content and teach in a traditional "lecture" style. Under these circumstances teaching is not interactive nor is the professor concerned about the learning needs of the student. Rather, the emphasis is on covering the content material.

Authentic learning in music means teaching students to do what real musicians do when they engage in the making of music. Musicians compose, analyze, perform and research. Children in music classes need to be engaged in musical activities and experiences that are the same as those of real musicians. These activities correlate to the National Standards for Music Education. Figure A (page 75) shows how the national standards are included in Dr. Dickson's 4MAT lesson. Authentic learning engages children in analysis, synthesis, and evaluation. These are higher order thinking (HOT) skills that are important for children in all subject domains. Figure B (page 76) shows where the higher order and lower level thinking skills occur in Dr. Dickson's lesson. Authentic learning also promotes substantive conversation. Children learn when they can discuss musical issues among themselves and with their teacher. These young students need to see the connections music has with the world outside the music class. For example, when schools wish to improve test scores in subjects like mathematics and science, or when business leaders want schools to produce future business leaders, they should look to the school music program. Although on the surface that may seem far fetched, it really is not. To be successful in mathematics, science, or business, students need to be problem solvers. They need to be able to look at a problem or a situation and find multiple solutions. In short, they need to be creative thinkers. It is in music and the other arts classes where children learn creative thinking. They discover that there are many correct answers and that there are a multiplicity of solutions. This is how music connects to the other subjects children learn in school. Connections to an integrated curriculum appear in Figure C (page 77). Finally, meeting each student's learning needs raises self-7esteem by providing opportunities for students to experience social support for their achievement.

The format of Dr. Dickson's lesson meets the criteria of authentic learning, engages higher order thinking skills, honors the diversity of learning styles within the class, and meets many of the national standards set by music educators. Using guided imagery, it begins by creating a problem that presents a need to know. Students are given the opportunity for conversation as they discuss their "most favorite place." The connection to the Brahms excerpt helps to show the power of music to engage the imagination—the composer's and the listener's. Students respond well to the lessons because of the diversity of activities and because Dr. Dickson alternated right brain teaching strategies with ones that utilized the left brain. The following formula is presented to assist you in writing 4MAT model lessons:

Improvisation

A. Choose a lesson plan from a lesson you have already taught. Analyze it against the criteria for a successful lesson presented above by Dr. Dickson. Analyze it against the national standards. Where are the weak points? Identify the higher order thinking (HOT) skills. Discuss with the class.

B. Transform your lesson into a 4MAT lesson. Add the missing steps. Correlate your objectives, activities, and assessments to the national standards and the criteria for a successful lesson. Identify the HOT skills. The Lesson Planning Model and blank lesson plan form is included at the conclusion of this chapter. You may duplicate it to use for your lesson planning. Note that 4MAT lessons may be written for classroom music at any grade level.

Recapitulation

A. Share your lesson with your colleagues and your teacher. Solicit feedback. Revise and refocus your lesson as appropriate.

B. Teach the new version.

4MAT® LESSON PLANNING MODEL
by Bernice McCarthy

Quadrant	Instructional Mode	Teacher Role	Instructional Strategy	PROCEDURE *Select a musical concept and then*
1	EXPERIENCE	MOTIVATE	DISCUSS	**1.** Engage the students in problem solving by creating an experience that will present a need to know. **(right mode)** **2.** Allow the students to share feelings and reflect. **(left mode)**
2	PRESENT	INFORM	LECTURE	**3.** Connect the experience to the musical concept using a different form such as poetry, drama, or dance. **(right mode)** **4.** Teach the musical concept. Present the evidence necessary for the students to solve the problem. **(left mode)**
3	PRACTICE	FACILITATE	DRILL	**5.** Collect the evidence and practice using the concept. A homework assignment might be included here. **(left mode)** **6.** Invite the students to find alternative solutions and new ways to use the information presented. Let them experiment. **(right mode)**
4	EXTEND	EVALUATE	DISCOVER	**7.** Provide the opportunity for students to reflect and evaluate their work. **(left mode)** **8.** Let the students teach themselves or present information to others. **(right mode)**

AUTHOR:
THEME:
GRADE LEVEL:

1.	EXPERIENCE
1. OBJECTIVE: ACTIVITY: ASSESSMENT:	
2. OBJECTIVE: ACTIVITY: ASSESSMENT:	
2.	PRESENT
3. OBJECTIVE ACTIVITY: ASSESSMENT:	
4. OBJECTIVE: ACTIVITY: ASSESSMENT:	

3.	PRACTICE
5. OBJECTIVE: ACTIVITY: ASSESSMENT:	
6. OBJECTIVE: ACTIVITY: ASSESSMENT:	
4	EXTEND
7. OBJECTIVE: ACTIVITY: ASSESSMENT:	
8. OBJECTIVE: Activity: ASSESSMENT:	

TI-TI-TA and Technology

Introduction

The next century will certainly be known as the age of technology. Computers enhanced with CD-ROM, interactive programs, modems, and easy access to the internet are changing the way children access information. Once used for tutorial enrichment, hardware and software are now integral in the delivery of instruction. More and more, music teachers are including technology in music classes. Utilizing sequencers, MIDI hook-ups and keyboards, computer technology opened the world of musical composition to students who previously would not have been able to create original compositions. Publishers began to produce supplemental materials for secondary school music theory programs, as well as utilitarian software for program management, marching band show design, and other administrative tasks.

This case presents a dilemma for first-year teacher Cooper Brightman. Although his immediate problem is finding a way to integrate technology into his Kodály curriculum, the situation is complicated by an interpersonal issue with his more experienced co-worker. Teachers are often faced with incorporating new ideas, techniques, and equipment into a program that seemingly works well as it is. When those changes are mandated by the central office, teachers have little choice but to comply.

Exposition

A. Read the Case: *TI-TI-TA and Technology*

Maya Angelou Middle School is located in the worst neighborhood of the city. It was built in 1993 and opened in September, 1994 after a long battle in the city over whether to build a new school in a neighborhood plagued by drugs and owned by two gangs, one African-American and the other Latino. Drugs are openly sold on street corners, nearly everyone carries some sort of weapon for protection, sex is for sale everywhere, and the streets are lined with bottles, broken glass, and other debris.

Many students at Angelou are children of teenage parents, seldom married, many on public assistance, many uneducated and unemployed. The devastating effects of substance abuse by mothers during pregnancy is clearly evident when one reviews the special education files and individual educational plans of the children at Angelou.

The city *did* build Angelou Middle School because of the commitment and vision of the new Superintendent, Dr. Ricardo Juarez. Dr. Juarez believed that going to school could make a difference in a child's life. He also believed that the school should be the focal point of a neighborhood. Dr. Juarez was hired because of his success in other urban districts, particularly for his gift for attracting business leaders in the community to provide supplemental financial support to the district. He chose the name Maya Angelou for the new middle school to honor the African-American poet, writer, and teacher chosen to speak at the Clinton Inauguration. He felt that her story would serve as an inspiration for the children and their families in the neighborhood.

Dr. Juarez was also a strong believer in the power of the arts in education. He understood the importance of aesthetics in education, of creativity, and he believed that children learn in a variety of styles and have a multiplicity of aptitudes (intelligences). He knew that the children at Angelou could be successful if teachers could tap into their potential beyond verbal and mathematical competencies. Juarez believed that the arts should be at the core of the middle school experience. He supported the new national standards developed by the consortium for arts education and wanted Angelou to embrace artistic expression in every discipline.

Cooper Brightman and Jasmine Carmen were hired to teach music at Maya Angelou Middle School when the school opened. Mr. Brightman had just graduated from college and this was his first job. He was a music education major at a small college in an ivy league town that emphasized the Kodály approach to teaching. He had a fine tenor voice and played jazz on the piano so well that he could easily have had a career in performance if he so desired. What he really wanted to do, though, was teach. In college, he was the president of the student chapter of MENC and attended the state conferences each of the years he was in school. He had a church job where he built a youth choir of seventy voices. Everybody loved him. But most importantly, he was a great teacher.

The other new hire, Jasmine Carmen, had been teaching for twenty-three years when she was transferred to this middle school. Ms. Carmen was also a singer who majored in vocal performance in college, with aspirations that she would have a successful career on the operatic stage. When it became evident to her that this was not going to happen, she reluctantly went back to college for a master's degree in education. She did her job each day, but it was clear that her heart just wasn't in it. In fact, one was not really sure that she even liked children. She taught from the Basal series books, went to the required in-service programs the district offered, and felt that her transfer to Maya Angelou Middle School was punishment for not having large performing groups in her previous school. "They're trying to get rid of me," she told Cooper on his first day. "But they'll have to carry me out, 'cause I'm not giving up my pension for nobody."

One afternoon, a year after the middle school had opened, the teachers were called to a special meeting in the auditorium.

It seemed that Superintendent Juarez was coming to make a special announcement. The teachers knew it was important, because beginning at noon the media trucks began parking their vans outside the building. Action News, Eyewitness News, and News Seven all sent representatives. At three o'clock Dr. Juarez arrived with his press representative and another very distinguished-looking African-American gentleman, impeccably dressed in an Armani suit. Clearly, something important was about to happen.

The principal introduced the superintendent and he approached the podium. Cooper was excited. Jasmine looked bored. "Ladies and gentlemen," he began, "let me thank you for coming today and welcome and express my appreciation to the media for also attending. I am pleased to introduce Adam Franklin, president of Franklin Publishing. Mr. Franklin is here to present this school with a check for three million dollars for the purchase of computers including hardware, peripherals, and software for use by teachers and students here at Maya Angelou Middle School. The funds will also be used to build a state-of-the-art video and sound studio and to wire the school so that each room has access to cable television and the internet. This will mean that Maya Angelou Middle School will have the most advanced and sophisticated technological capabilities of any middle school in the world! Mr. Franklin has pledged to support in-service training for faculty and staff as well as for parents in the neighborhood and has donated 500 computers to be distributed to families of children at Angelou who apply for them."

The room fell deadly silent. Then one by one the faculty began to applaud, then cheer, then stand. Some cried, and some like Jasmine Carmen looked in fear and disbelief. What was going on here, she wondered? Were they turning the school into a science and technology magnet? What was going to happen to the arts? Why wasn't the faculty consulted? Is this just another example of top-down decision-making that never was successful? Was this going to be another one of those plans that fizzled after a year or so? Could she transfer back to her other school where nobody bothered her or cared what she did? And what about having all this equipment in the school? Would that motivate more crime? Would the school become a target for robbery, theft, looting, and vandalism? How could she possibly integrate technology into the music program? And what about Cooper? How could he integrate technology into a Kodály curriculum? She knew it just couldn't be done.

B. In cooperative groups discuss each of the following:
1. What are the issues? Who are the stakeholders?
2. What is the role of technology in music education? How can it enhance the curriculum?
3. Check the national standards. What are the implications for technology?
4. How can technology enhance a Kodály curriculum?

Development

A. Write a position paper describing your stance on the issue of technology in the school music program. Will computers depersonalize education? How much should be mandated by the federal government? Argue your case.

B. Horace Mann, a nineteenth-century pioneer in school reform, argued that the organization of a common school system would promote economic development. Some would argue that schooling as a means of developing human capital has become the most important goal of the educational system in the twentieth century.

In nineteenth and twentieth centuries, the idea was that education improved the skills of individuals and made them more productive members of society. From this increased productivity, economic growth would be enhanced. In this context, the money we invest in education will pay off as an increase in the economic wealth of our society.

Schools were under pressure to meet two demands. First, students must be provided with the tools they need to obtain a job. Secondly, employers demand education in order to improve the quality of the work force.

As a reaction to these issues of societal need, the culture of our schools has changed. A curriculum of character education, civics, and practical skills has been replaced with a course of study that provides the necessary credentials for getting a job. This idea shaped the modern high school curriculum, and, most dramatically, the concept of tracking. Students going on to higher education studied for a college diploma. Those planning to work after graduation earned general or vocational credentials. Schools also expanded their extra and co-curricular activities to include clubs, sports, assemblies, and student government. Such activities were designed to teach American youth how to cooperate in an industrial and corporate society.

In 1892 the National Education Association (NEA) formed the Committee of Ten. Charles Eliot, President of Harvard University, was the chair. The committee was charged with standardizing requirements for admission to college. From this task, important questions were raised about the goals of secondary education. For example, should high schools track students? Should the programs of study be different for those planning to attend college? These are significant questions because they strike at the core of the role of education in a democratic society. Also, issues of access surfaced which still today have not been resolved. Charges of elitism were raised against the committee. Issues of social class were not considered. It appears that the committee widened the gap between the rich and the poor.

In 1964, Edward Krug wrote about social efficiency as the most predominant school of thought in influencing the development of the high school curriculum. However, by labeling students and tracking them, the division of classes was only perpetuated.

Schools today are changing again in response to human capital. Political and business leaders are very concerned with the future of American youth. Specifically, they question whether our youth will be able to compete in a global economy. Alternatives to public schools, such as charter schools, home schooling, and private school vouchers, bring some solutions. Additionally, block scheduling and learning communities within large high school buildings are examples of other solutions. The emphasis on developing thinking skills, problem-solving strategies, and cooperation now hold a prominent position in the curriculum. Similar to Jonathan Kozal, some point out the inequalities in opportunity, program, and access. His book, *Savage Inequalities* (1991), presents case studies comparing neighboring districts. He concludes that it all comes down to money and power.

Also, some critical theorists claim that schools foster reproduction theory. This theory contends that rich children go to better schools and attend college. Thus, they become more successful. Contrarily, poor children, who are often minorities, go to inferior schools, and therefore, they do not have the opportunities to improve their class status. In other words, schooling perpetuates our class system. Neighborhood schools, forced busing, clustering, and freedom of choice are alternatives which some districts have adopted in an attempt to break this cycle. These strategies have not been successful. Although many schools now see the flaws in tracking, they attempt to provide support services for students with specialized needs. However, very little has changed. Tyack and others (1974) conclude that in the late nineteenth and early twentieth centuries, education was controlled by business and power structures. Many feel it still is.

The issue of emerging technologies is at the top of any list of priorities for the future. Distance learning, where students are at multiple sites linked by satellite television, and resources now available on the internet are rapidly changing the way instruction is delivered. President Clinton's promise to connect every classroom in America to the information superhighway provides further evidence that education must embrace technology and move forward.

Questions abound: How will this look? Will the metaphor change from schools as communities to schools as learning sites? Will resources on the internet mean that more students will find it desirable to learn at home? Will the role of the teacher shift from motivator, informer, facilitator, and evaluator to technician? Will the fact that students can learn via electronics, conceivably at any time they wish, change the way the day is structured? Will schooling shift to "round the clock," providing options for students to do other things during the traditional school hours? Will artificial intelligence and cloning make it possible to reconstruct the minds of those in past eras? Will a student be able to have Mozart evaluate her piano performance? Will technology enhance or restrict access to education by minorities and the poor? Who will be the powerful and privileged?

For students in the poor urban districts, the answers are frightening. One hopes that distance learning will provide increased access to quality instruction for many more children. Instead it may just widen the gap between the rich and the poor. Although government promises are encouraging, they are politically based. Often a new administration takes power and then priorities change.

Historically, education moves in cycles. In 1936, Edgar B. Gordon a professor of music at University of Wisconsin in Madison, wrote:

> As an accessory to many of the newer forms of musical activity, the radio is now playing an important part. Just how far it may be employed to supplant the personal presence of a teacher is yet to be determined . . . . The popularity of the radio as a substitute for the piano in the home for a time threatened the entire piano industry. Fortunately, there seems to be a reaction in favor of the piano. It is to be hoped that this may continue until that instrument is once more restored to its proper place in the American home. For it is around the piano, the

fireplace, and the dining table that much of family life centers.

When Robert Moog introduced the synthesizer in the 1960's, many predicted it would be the end of live music. Neither has happened. People still play the piano in their homes and go to live concerts, and symphony orchestras continue to perform and record.

Technology is another tool, and yet another way to reach children and teach to their individual differences. It can provide the enrichment for those children who move at a faster pace than the class, and remediation for those children who need a bit extra to succeed.

Technophobics, like Jasmine Carmen, will be left behind. Her fears that computers will replace the one-on-one human contact of the classroom teacher are unfounded. One can easily speculate that if Mozart were alive today, he would be writing on state-of-the-art equipment. So would Bach and Beethoven and Wagner and Stravinsky. Louis V. Gerstner, Jr., the chief executive of IBM, expressed it best. When speaking to the 1997 graduating class at Wake Forest University he said, "Computers are magnificent tools for the realization of our dreams, but they will never replace the dreamers. No machine can replace the human spark: spirit, compassion, love, and understanding." Technology is here and we must embrace it. It does and will provide options that allow children to explore creativity and to dream. After all, isn't that what music education is all about?

Improvisation

A. Make a chart of the various ways technology is integrated into your life each day. Begin with ATM machines. Then make of list of the ways technology might be routinely integrated into a school music program. Don't forget the overhead projector—that's technology, too.

B. Create a lesson that integrates technology. Your methodology need not be limited to the Kodály approach.

Recapitulation

A. Peer review your lesson. Does it meet the criteria for a successful lesson present on page 77? Does it meet national standards? Is technology integral to the lesson content or to the lesson methodology?

B. Peer teach your lesson.

Fiddler on the Fence

Introduction

Dedicated teachers will say that their students come first. Seeing the joy on their faces and the light in their eyes provides the motivation to keep teachers going day after day. As economic times become tough, and as issues of school reform force school districts to make difficult decisions, it is those smiling faces and bright eyes staring up at loving teachers that make it all worthwhile.

Raymond Carlson was just this kind of teacher. Working long hours and often on weekends, he built a music program that was respected in the community. For his efforts, he was rewarded with loyal and adoring students. They would do anything for him and he, in turn, would do anything for them. He felt pride and accomplishment when they did well, and he agonized with them when they did not make the grade. Parents often said that Mr. Carlson was a role model for his students. He could always be counted on to "do the right thing." However, when the teacher's union went on strike the week of the school musical, Raymond Carlson was faced with a dilemma when doing the right thing was not so easily defined.

Exposition

A. Consider the dilemma in the Case: *Fiddler on the Fence*

Raymond Carlson continued briefing Lisa, his student teacher on her eighth-grade theory lesson as they walked into the teacher workroom in the basement of Grouse Mountain Middle School. A few teachers gathered near the table where donuts and coffee somehow magically appeared every Friday morning.

To meet Raymond, one would surely be impressed by his gregarious personality, and he seemed eager to greet his colleagues and perhaps even chat about the weather. However, on this particular morning, Lisa noticed the reception from some of his co-workers to be lukewarm at best. The other teachers went about their business of the day and talked among themselves, but they would scarcely make eye contact with Raymond. Only Brenda Peterson from the English department really stopped to acknowledge that he was even in the room.

"They're certainly not overly friendly around here, are they, Mr. Carlson?" Lisa seemed puzzled about the awkward exchange that had just taken place downstairs.

"Well . . ." Ray Carlson explained, "I guess that's partially my fault. It seems I made a few enemies awhile back."

"You? Enemies?" Lisa was puzzled. "You're one of the most easy-going people I know."

"Well, Lisa, the story goes something like this . . ." Mr. Carlson continued to tell the story of his arrival at Grouse Mountain Middle School nearly seven years ago. "My first year here I was hired to fill the maternity leave for Alicia Bozarth, the previous band director here at Grouse Mountain. She said when she left that she probably wouldn't be back, but they hired me on a temporary contract just the same. Anyway, it began as a very good year, especially considering I was a first-year teacher. That was, of course, until the walkout."

"The walkout? I don't understand?" Lisa was still trying to figure out what this all had to do with the cold shoulder treatment downstairs. "What walkout?"

97

Ray continued, "It seems the teachers had been working for over a year without a contract. This meant nothing to me at the time. I was just happy to have a job! But in any case, it all finally came to a head on one snowy day in March. The teachers association set the deadline for a week from Friday. If the district did not meet their demands, then the teachers would go out on strike."

"That sounds horrible!" Lisa was genuinely sympathetic. "So what happened next?"

"You haven't yet heard the worst of it." Ray was becoming more emotional now. "You see, the spring musical was set to open the first weekend in April. You know Brenda Peterson. Well, she was the drama teacher then, and a guy named Reg Thomas worked with the singers. I was in charge of the orchestra and building the sets."

"So did all the teachers walk out? Did you go on with the show?" Lisa hung on every word.

"It was not quite that simple." Ray said emptily, "Yes, the teachers did walk out on strike. But what was I to do with the show? The sets were nearly finished, and the orchestra had been rehearsing for three months. The blocking was done and the cast members had already sold tickets to every friend and relative they could find."

"So, you did go on with the show?" Lisa was hopeful.

"Not exactly." Ray's eyebrow furled as he recalled that fateful day. "When the teachers walked out, Brenda Peterson, Reg Thomas, and I all walked out with them. We felt that we needed to stand behind our colleagues and the organization that represents us! Reg was the most adamant as he could remember signing his first contract for an annual salary of $6000.00. He gave a lot of credit to the teachers' association for making wages more competitive since he began his career just twelve years ago."

"All three of us walked the line for two days as anxious students came to bring us food and moral support while inquiring about the fate of the nearly completed musical. By the end of the first week, it was clear that there was no settlement in sight, and that's when the trouble began."

"It sounds awful enough already," provoked Lisa. "How could it get worse?"

"The three of us, Reg, Brenda, and I, decided to have a meeting with the students and talk about the musical to discuss possible options. Reg just wanted to tell them *too bad, maybe next year*. But Brenda and I felt the students were getting trapped in the middle; and when all was said and done, they would be the losers. In the end, Brenda and I crossed the picket line to try and save the show and be with the students. Reg continued to walk the line and the rest of us picked up his part of the job."

"So how long did the strike last?" Lisa sounded disheartened.

"Nearly six weeks," said Ray despondently. "And in the end, the musical was canceled anyway. Merchants called and refused to let us hand out programs that had already been printed containing their ads, and parents were afraid to cross the picket line fearing retaliation once their children were back in the classroom. Brenda and I stayed in school with the students to the bitter end. But by the time it was all over, the students had pretty much lost heart, not just in the musical, but in school, too."

Lisa paused trying to understand. "Did the teachers win?"

Ray stepped out of his narrative role and back into that of a mentor teacher. "In a situation like this, nobody wins! Not the teachers, not the school board, and especially not the students."

"If it happened again, would you do the same thing?" Lisa searched for answers.

Ray explained, "Well, with the collective bargaining process that's currently in place, hopefully it never will. However, the issues in a case like this are many. As a new teacher in a temporary position, I thought it would be a smart move to come back to work, and after all, I did it for the students. But to this day there are teachers that will hardly even acknowledge me when passing in the hallway."

"That's rather childish, don't you think?" Lisa accused.

"Yes, and no." Ray came to their defense. "I came back to

protect my personal concerns while acting upon a premise that I believed in very deeply. Those who walked out believed just as deeply in their cause; and in fact, they will tell you that even *I* have continued to benefit from their willingness to walk the line on *my* behalf. The fact is, they're right!"

"So, you're sorry you came back to work?" Lisa was having trouble choosing sides.

"I didn't say that," Raymond jumped in. "I'm sorry it had to happen. I may have saved my job and even helped a few students, but I'll never know for certain how many bridges I burned in my effort to do the right thing."

    B. As a class, discuss the following:
1. What is the role of the teachers' union in the contemporary public school?
   a. What positive attributes does the teachers' association bring to the school community?
   b. What are some of the less positive perceptions of the teachers' association? What is the NEA and how is it perceived by the public at large?
2. Given a situation like this, would you go back to work or wait out the storm?
3. If students are the teacher's first priority, what would be a possible win/win solution for the students' needs and concerns?

Development

    A. When dealing with an ethical dilemma such as *Fiddler on the Fence*, one might consider the difference between the principle of benefit maximization and the principle of equal respect. By considering what would benefit the most people, one applies the principle of benefit maximization. In the case of *Fiddler*, what would be in the best interests of the most people, (i.e., the students, the parents, the community vs. the cause of the teachers on strike). An absolutist position such as the principle of equal respect says that everyone is of equal value. Therefore, we must consider the consequences for each side equally.

Divide yourselves into two groups. One half shall debate the principle of benefit maximization in this case, arguing that it is in the interest of the most people to have the show go on. The other half shall counter with the principle of equal respect, that is, it is wrong to go against the strike, no matter what the consequences. Your teacher shall be the judge and jury.

B. An understanding of the role and history of the teacher's union is extremely important to the analysis of this case. By regulating working conditions, ensuring fair salaries, medical and other benefits, and by providing legal aid for teachers in litigation, they have enabled teachers to maintain a reasonable standard of living. Today the average teacher's salary in Pennsylvania, for instance, is more than the average combined household income of that state. As the public perception of teachers (and teaching in general) changes, unions have fought to ensure that educators are treated fairly. At the same time, there are those who feel the teacher's unions have outlived their usefulness. Arguments that teachers are overpaid for short hours and long vacations repeatedly surface amidst debates regarding standards for teachers and education. Understanding how the unions have evolved should help you sift through these complex issues so that you might see where each side is coming from.

Before teachers began to organize with one another, the prevailing mindset was that teaching was a career predominantly for women. Teachers at the end of the nineteenth century were victims of low wages and inadequate retirement funds. Women found themselves at the mercy of a scientific management model that favored male administrators and looked to the female teaching force as second-class citizens. Teachers were at the bottom of the chain of command. They had no influence on educational policy or the improvement of salary and working conditions.

In Atlanta, Chicago, and New York, teachers organized to raise the economic standards of the teaching profession. This was the beginning of the union movement in education. Early in the twentieth century, the teachers' associations were conservative. However as the associations linked with labor unions, they began to gain political clout and slowly change their social status. When the unions became stronger, the gap widened between the teaching force and the administration.

The most significant impact on the development of unions was the rift between the American Federation of Teachers (AFT) and the National Education Association (NEA). The NEA was formed in 1857 to upgrade the teaching profession. By the end of the nineteenth century it was powerful enough to influence educational policy. Comprising the largest segment of the teaching profession, women surprisingly were excluded from membership until the 1950's when the federal government assumed a more visible role in leading national educational policy.

The AFT was formed in 1916 when the Chicago Federation of Men Teachers and Federation of Women Teachers, with local unions from Indiana, New York, Pennsylvania, and Washington, DC, organized to pool resources and affiliated with the American Federation of Labor (AFL).

Later, the Depression caused the political climate to shift. Pertaining to education, the economy forced school administrators, school boards, and local citizens to reexamine government spending on education. Resultantly, that which had been considered commonplace came under scrutiny as programs like kindergarten and vocational education became identified as "fads and frills." Meanwhile, in 1935 the Wagner Act was passed. This significant legislation, signed by President Franklin D. Roosevelt, gave employees the right to strike. This was a major victory for the unions. Historically, the public sector was expected to earn less than people working in private industry. As a result of the enactment of the Wagner Act, teachers found protection in the right to strike which would prove invaluable in the years that followed as teacher salaries would eventually match or even surpass their counterparts in other industries.

By 1946, teachers started to look toward a process called "collective bargaining." This process called upon employers and employees to meet in a process designed to work out a mutual agreement regarding salaries, benefits, and a myriad of issues related to working conditions. From the start, the American Federation of Teachers (AFT) and the National Education Association (NEA) acted as representatives for the teachers' unions. A landmark case in 1961 involved New York City teachers who agreed to affiliate with the AFT. This resulted in a strike which produced their first viable contract. Following this success all of the major urban areas began to engage in collective bargaining. Even though some state laws prohibited this form of negotiation, they couldn't afford to eliminate the process since teachers were in demand and the risk of losing them was too great.

Finally, President John F. Kennedy signed the Executive Order #10988 in 1962 which gave federal employees the right to bargain with their employers. Gains made by the AFT in the early 1960's were great although their approach was quite different than that of the NEA. The AFT took their model from private industry. The NEA still resisted collective bargaining. They felt teachers were professionals, and bargaining was for blue-collar workers. Now, however, there is hardly a district that does not participate in some form of collective bargaining at least to some extent. Today, it is not uncommon to have a mediator involved to facilitate the process and keep the process positive and moving forward. Many districts specifically credit this process for encouraging smooth negotiations while keeping teachers off the picket line.

There are as many different perspectives of the role and importance of unionized labor as there are people in the work force. One would be hard-pressed to argue against the accomplishments made by such organizations over the past century, but the modus operandus can often be a point of controversy. A young teacher will sometimes take the perspective, "why should I care? I just want to teach." That was certainly the driving force behind

Raymond Carlson. The failure to confront such issues creates a confrontation within itself. Further, regardless of one's personal position, it will be useful to maintain at least an awareness of the prevailing public climates towards such issues as well. You may find it difficult to rally community fervor and support if there is a general disregard for public education and its perceived values. Here are two considerations that are closely related to the role of teachers' unions in today's society:

1. In the public school, teachers are uniformly governed by the teachers' unions. Salaries, hiring practices, and issues regarding tenure are all a result of ongoing collective bargaining agreements. While many herald this as a strength of the union, there are limitations implied as well. Salary increases based on merit are rarely seen. Many districts are unable to hire a teacher with more than five years experience at a competitive wage. Practices such as these are coming under scrutiny as charter schools and voucher programs continue to take hold around the nation.

2. Administrators are not members of the teachers' union. In fact, in the case of a walkout, they will be the first called upon to work in the classroom. If negotiations become tense, lasting damage can affect the ongoing relationship with your administration. However, it is helpful to remember that most administrators were once teachers as well.

Improvisation

A. Interview a public school teacher. Ask what his or her position would be relative to *Fiddler on the Fence*.

B. At home, think about your values, the issues in *Fiddler on the Fence* , the principles of benefit maximization and equal respect. Then, write a professional ethics code.

or

With a partner, assume that you are the parent of the child playing the lead part in the production of *Fiddler* and your partner is the child playing the lead role. Assume further that the production is canceled. Role-play the conversation.

Recapitulation

A. In class, share your assignments.

B. Assume that the production goes forward; however, the teachers picket the performance. Write a speech that you will give to the audience before the performance begins.

Yikes, an A+ in Band!

Introduction

The inherent quality that separates music from many other activity-based opportunities for our students is the process itself. For most of us, the euphoria of performance is second only to those moments of discovery and shared experience that occur spontaneously within the rehearsal. It is that experience that we hope our students will carry with them as they go on, in hopes that they will one day return to music later in life, with a view of music as a vehicle to a deeper understanding of the human condition and the world around us. If this is to take place, the educator must be empowered, if not obligated, to nurture and stretch each individual to the best of his/her collective ability. Assessment is pivotal in this process as it will ultimately determine what is worth teaching, how it should be taught, and how it will be reflected in the musicians we train and inspire.

There are many issues involved in grading students in music education classes. Attitude, effort, and behavior are often at the top of the list. What complicates the matter is the phenomenon of natural talent. Should students who try hard but have little ability get good grades? Or should all students be measured against a universal standard? Whatever teachers decide, they must be accountable. That is to say, they must be able to produce a criteria for determining grades and be able to provide justification.

In the scenario that follows, Mr. Rooney's grading policy is challenged by concerned parents. How he defends his actions will reflect not only his philosophy of teaching, but his personal and professional ethics as well.

Exposition

A. Read the Case: *Yikes, an A+ in Band!*

Danny transferred to Richfield High when his family moved the summer before he finished at Northwood Middle School. They moved because Danny was a trombone/euphonium player and the music program at Northwood High had suffered severe budget cuts. The band at Northwood was small and did not play the caliber of literature they played at Richfield. The Northwood H.S. Marching Band was the joke of the city, and the jazz ensemble was an embarrassment as well.

On the other hand, Richfield had a reputation for strong academics and a school board that valued the arts. Located in Boston's prestigious North Shore area, Richfield was a professional community where parents took an active interest in their children and the schools. The band was large, the marching unit consistently won awards, and the jazz ensemble was recognized as one of the finest throughout the state.

By the time Danny was ready to start at Richfield High, the president of the parent booster organization, TEMPO (To Encourage Musical Performing Organizations), had rather abruptly decided to step down to pursue other interests. Danny's father assumed the role of board president, and his mother became actively involved in many of the fund-raising activities. In the meantime, Danny was already taking euphonium lessons with a New England University graduate student who was recommended by the chair of the brass department. In addition, he was also an internationally-known concert artist.

Danny was apprehensive about his new school. However,

when he arrived at the first band rehearsal and found in his folder the Holst *Second Suite in F for Military Band* (the one with the famous euphonium solo), he was thrilled.

Things seemed to be going well for Danny, especially in band. He loved the marching band and had auditioned for the district band. He was practicing a good bit, too. He wanted to have that Holst solo nailed in case Ben, the senior euphonium player, couldn't play it. He even found time to sell twenty-three cases of oranges for the fall fund-raiser and continued to make many new friends.

By the end of the first marking period before the mid-term grades came out, things were looking good. Then reports cards arrived. Danny had an A+ in band!

His parents were stunned. How could a freshman get an A+ in band for the first marking period? Was there no room for improvement? How could Danny sustain an A+ for three more years (fifteen more marking periods)? What was going on? Danny's parents thought they should discuss this with Mr. Rooney, the band director. Perhaps there would be a few moments after the next TEMPO meeting on Monday night.

Mr. Rooney had been the band director at Richfield for over thirty-five years during which he had built a reputation for excellence. During most of that time he had been the department chair as well. He had a strong personality. Students either loved him or hated him; but either way, everyone respected him and shared in the pride of the music program. A few years ago, however, things began to change. The state passed "Proposition 2 1/2" that limited funding for schools resulting in severe budget cuts for every school in the state.

At Richfield, the superintendent decided to consolidate the music, art, and industrial arts departments into one department of Fine and Applied Arts. The school hired Ms. Renard as the chair of the entire department, not only "dethroning" Mr. Rooney, but also severely impacting the identity of the music department, too. Mr. Rooney took it very hard. He and some of the parents fervently fought the superintendent's so called "solutions," but to no avail. Not only was he angry about losing his administrative position, he was also offended by having to work under the supervision of someone half his age who barely knew the needs of a successful music program. People who knew Rooney for many years noticed a change in him almost overnight. Students told stories about the day Rooney screamed at Susan Parker in front of the entire band because her flute was being repaired. They also remembered the day he stuck his baton into the wall behind the podium after the xylophone player missed a cue. Some said he had a breakdown. Others felt he was just burned out and should move on.

However, Danny's parents felt that as long as the quality of the music program was not being compromised, they could put up with his temper tantrums and erratic behavior.

Monday night's TEMPO meeting began with the traditional reading of the minutes and the latest report from the football game popcorn sale coordinator. The new department chair, Ms. Renard, routinely attended these meetings, but rarely spoke out. Having only been at the school for a year, she seemed mostly interested in monitoring what happened in this program which continued to involve so many students and parents.

During the meeting Mr. Rooney gave the Band Director's report. As part of his "state of the union" type address, he nonchalantly mentioned that first-quarter grades were issued last week. This caught Renard's attention, who rather bluntly responded to Mr. Rooney's report. "So do most of the students get an A in music classes, Mr. Rooney?"

"Well no . . ." Rooney was rather shocked by the question.

Danny's father was reluctant to put the band director on the spot, but he also was curious. "Well, Danny got an A+ in band." He proceeded, "On what was that based?"

"Well," Rooney began, "Danny works hard, he takes private lessons in Boston, he sold the most oranges in the fund-raising sale, he auditioned for the all-district band, and his parents are active in TEMPO. I just wanted to reward him for his dedication."

Ms. Renard came to the rescue in an effort to avert the fall-out she apparently had begun. "This is definitely worth further discussion, but I'm not sure this is the time or the place." Ms. Renard continued, "Perhaps a few of us could meet in my office later this week to explore this in greater depth. Would that be okay with you, Mr. Rooney?"

B. Complete the following activities:
1. In class, discuss the following questions:
   a. What criteria did Mr. Rooney use to determine Danny's grade?
   b. Does Mr. Rooney have a grading policy? If so, what do you think it looks like?
   c. What is good about Mr. Rooney's "criteria?" How is it effective in motivating students?
   d. What is lacking in Mr. Rooney's policy? What is it that he should be evaluating?
   e. What are some common misconceptions about grading in music performing ensembles? What are some typical responses you might get from a parent or an administrator when discussing a grading policy for a music class?

2. It is 3:30 on Thursday afternoon in Ms. Renard's office. The following people are in attendance at the meeting regarding grading concerns in the music department. In small groups, choose a role and play out the follow-up meeting regarding Rooney's grading policy.

Danny	the euphonium player and seller of oranges
Danny's father	concerned parent and president of TEMPO
Ms. Renard	the Fine/Applied Arts Department Chair
Mr. Rooney	a veteran music teacher

Development

A. Following the presentation in cooperative learning groups, take a moment to reflect and identify the main focus of the issue at hand. Write a limerick that identifies the problem in Mr. Rooney's classroom.

For example, if we were to describe a student that was very "booksmart" but unable to draw logical conclusions that would allow him to make connections to the real world, the limerick might read like this:

> There once was a boy named O'Sage
> Who solved calculus quests in a rage
> But when driving, alas,
> He ran out of gas
> He was quick, but could not read a gauge.

B. Evaluation and Assessment

There are many issues that make the assessment process complex for music educators. How can we be consistent and fair to students with varying abilities? What about the student with lesser talent who is an excellent fund-raiser or consistently helps out with menial tasks? Will a tough grading policy scare students away from the program? Do we want to be known as the teacher who gives "easy A's?"

Teachers of ensembles are always listening and responding to what is taking place within the rehearsal, devising solutions for problems like intonation and articulation, and making constant evaluative decisions to guide the students toward a successful performance. The teacher in this role is held accountable for these innumerable decisions as the performing ensemble is ultimately judged by the listening public.

The National Standards provide some help. The standards in music education are very specific in terms of what competencies a student should be able to demonstrate and perform.

The MENC National Standards in music education are as follows:

1. Singing alone and with others, a varied repertoire of music.
2. Performing on instruments, alone and with others, a varied repertoire of music.
3. Improvising melodies, variations, and accompaniments.
4. Composing and arranging music within specified guidelines.
5. Reading and notating and describing music.
6. Listening to, analyzing, and describing music.
7. Evaluating music and music performances.
8. Understanding relationships between music, the other arts, and disciplines outside the arts.
9. Understanding music in relation to history and culture.

    (from National Standards for Arts Education, MENC, 1994)

If standards in musical performance are not mandated by the school district, it will be up to the individual teacher to decide exactly which standards, if any, are to be embraced within the ensemble. As in most cases, the music teacher is the specialist able to teach in that subject area on any given campus. This sovereignty implies a power for each teacher to make these kind of curricular decisions.

Will there be individual testing? Should students be required to understand the theoretical complexities of what is being performed? Should time be spent on sight-reading or will there be numerous sectionals and part tapes to enable the students to learn the pitches regardless of their ability to read? How will each be weighted into a final grade?

Learning is said to be authentic when it meets the following five criteria:

1. *Promotes substantive conversation.*
   Children understand when they are able to take information learned in one context and use it in a new and different context. For learning to be long lasting, children

must be given opportunities to engage in conversations where they demonstrate that they can use the information in a context.

2. *Focuses on depth of knowledge rather than breadth.*
Too often teachers try to cover too much material. It is far better, the research tells us, to cover less breadth of material; rather, cover smaller amounts of material in greater depth.

3. *Promotes higher order thinking.*
Part of teaching is to engage children in activities where they must analyze, synthesize, and evaluate or critique. These higher level skills are necessary in music as in other subjects for true learning to occur.

4. *Makes connections to the world beyond the classroom.*
Students must see that what they are learning has some use outside the classroom. That is to say, in music classes, children learn to do what real musicians (the musicers) do when they engage in the act of music-making (musicing).

5. *Provides children with support when they achieve.*
All children need to be recognized for their accomplishments. This nurtures self-esteem and provides the motivation for children to achieve and meet high standards and high expectations.

If learning is authentic, then assessment must also be authentic. Traditional tests, while they serve a specific purpose, do not always measure the total picture. More common in enlightened music classes are portfolios because they promote authentic learning. Portfolios document authentic musical behaviors such as performing, practicing, reflective thinking, studying and researching, composing, and improvising. They emphasize process over time being as important as the final product. Further, portfolios accommodate multiple solutions to musical problems and individualize learning. Portfolios promote conversation. Students with their teachers select materials to go into the portfolio and meet together to evaluate the portfolio.

Portfolios provide a mechanism for monitoring and promoting learning progress in skill attainment and creative growth.

In an ensemble environment, portfolios allow the conductor or teacher to connect to each student on a personal level. Through the student journal, each member has a direct line to the conductor, and the conductor can monitor student progress and provide remedial instruction, redirection, and intervention where necessary.

If journals and portfolios are among the most common tools for authentic assessment, one must also have an approach to measure the overall success of a student's progress. A rubric is such a tool that helps to convert subjective evidence into an objective grade. The rubric will outline several areas of competencies which will correspond to the learning goals. Referring to the rubric below, notice that each of these areas calls upon the instructor to know the student well enough to find out what individual qualities he or she brings to the program. Many of these categories will ultimately be influenced by the success demonstrated through more objective tools of measurement, such as part testing and seat challenges. However, even those might be viewed through the knowledge of the particular student's aptitude, thereby creating a more accurate picture of the student's progress and depth of knowledge and not just measuring his or her ability to participate at a level of proficiency which may have existed before entering the program.

One way to design a rubric is to define the minimum expectation of the task. The minimum becomes 3 on a scale of 5 - 1. Then, set the criteria above the expectation and below it.

RUBRIC FOR PERFORMANCE CLASSES and ENSEMBLES

Student Name _____

Date _____

Attendance

3. Student meets the established attendance policy and arrives to class or rehearsal on time with music prepared.

2. Student is occasionally late or is absent frequently.

1. Student has a poor attendance record and rarely shows evidence of preparation.

Comment:

Performance

3. Student performs at potential and exceeds the expectations of the instructor.

2. Student performs at an appropriate level according to developmental ability and meets the minimum expectations of the class or ensemble and the instructor.

1. Student performs below potential and does not meet the expectations of the class or ensemble and the instructor.

Comment:

Musical Growth

3. Student demonstrates musical growth that exceeds the expectations of the instructor.

2. Student demonstrates musical growth sufficient to meet the minimum expectations of the instructor.

1. Student does not meet the expectations of the instructor or the objectives of the class or ensemble.

Comment:

Technical Proficiency

3. Student exceeds expectations of the instructor relative to technical proficiency appropriate to the developmental level of the class or ensemble.

2. Student shows growth in technical proficiency appropriate to the expectations of the instructor.

1. Student does not meet the instructor's expectations for the class or ensemble.

Comment:

Critical Thinking

3. Student regularly questions, probes and processes material above the levels usually expected.

2. Student provides evidence that demonstrates an ability to analyze, synthesize and evaluate.

1. Student provides little or no evidence of the ability to think critically.

Comment:

Musical Thinking

3. Student excels in areas of aesthetic perception.

2. Student is able to use musical thinking to analyze and solve musical problems.

1. Student rarely engages musical thinking to solve musical problems.

Comment:

Class or Ensemble Culture and Community

3. Student takes a leadership role in the class or ensemble and is actively involved in promoting its goals and activities.

2. Student is a cooperative member of the class or ensemble.

1. Student does not contribute positively to the culture or community of the class or ensemble.

Comment:

Total points earned _____ Course Grade _____

Instructor's Signature _____

Improvisation

A. Review the National Standards as set forth by the Music Educators National Conference. Identify those which you deem most important to a student's success in your music program. Develop an activity that exemplifies each standard to which you will teach. Include a description of the process of assessing competency in that standard at a particular level.

B. Discuss how each might be assessed.

Recapitulation

A. Review the case study about Danny and Mr. Rooney. Given the facts in the case, develop a rubric for Mr. Rooney. In cooperative groups, share your rubrics. Come up with a group rubric.

B. Present your rubrics to the entire class.

No Way Out

Introduction

Nearly all of us can remember touring with the high school performance ensemble, even if it was simply a day trip to a local music festival. Without question, the rewards are innumerable, not only musically but also for simply forming an ensemble into a successful team. It may be one of the few times during the year where the students actually get to know one another, and that in turn will help them work together in the classroom.

However, traveling with a group of students brings additional responsibilities for the teacher in charge. These extend beyond musical decisions and into value judgments. These issues will ultimately be a reflection of the goals and priorities of our programs, along with the educational philosophy.

Leslie Burella worked diligently to create a program that would encourage her students to maximize their potential in musicianship and performance. Yet in the end, she is forced to reexamine those very activities that were meant to create goals and motivation, but created havoc instead.

Exposition

A. Read the Case: *No Way Out*

The candle sales, the play-a-thons, and the flea market in the pouring rain were worth it. Even though the competition was still four days away, the North Hills High School Orchestra already felt like world champions. This would be a major victory for Ms. Leslie Burella who had come to North Hills just three years ago to resurrect the string program. She was certain the community would rally with support and enthusiasm if only she could return with the coveted Grand Sweepstakes Trophy from the Florida Orchestral Directors League.

After all, that was the guiding motivation for the whole idea of attending the festival in the first place. "Motivation to attain excellence is what it's all about," Ms. Burella would tell the anxious boosters at the Monday night meetings. "We have to set standards and goals for our students—give them something to work for that they can accomplish as a team!" Their successful performance would prove that Ms. Burella was right!

Finally the moment of truth was at hand. It was day four of the six-day tour: competition day! Last night's performance had gone exceedingly well. The Grieg *Holberg Suite* was exquisite. The players were really grasping the nuance of each of the dance-like movements. However, the crowning achievement was the Wieniawski Violin Concerto No. 4 featuring their own student virtuoso, Rachel Dearborn.

Always a serious student, Rachel was a strong candidate for valedictorian of her senior class. Her accomplished musicianship was no exception. She had an extraordinary talent that set her apart from the average high school string player, even as an incoming freshman. The Wieniawski was her piece! She could play it cold, and Ms. Burella knew this would be an important part of the chemistry in leading the orchestra successfully through the competitive events.

This Saturday morning was unseasonably chilly for a spring day in Florida. But Ms. Burella didn't mind. As the students boarded the buses, she could attribute her pacing about the parking lot to the cold, rather than the nervous energy that might undermine the confidence she had so carefully instilled in her students.

"Ms. Burella, may I speak with you?" Amanda was another valuable player in the North Hills High School Orchestra. Having dreams of one day becoming a music teacher, she had come to assume the role of Ms. Burella's assistant in both rehearsal and organizational duties.

"What's up Amanda?" Ms. Burella was still absorbed with the musical agenda of the coming day.

"Well," Amanda hesitated, "people are talking."

"Sure, about what?" Ms. Burella was only half paying attention as she continued to mentally count the students getting on the bus.

Amanda continued, "Some students were drinking last night."

The color quickly faded from Ms. Burella's face. She paused. "Are you sure?"

"I feel horrible!" Amanda was near tears. "Just check out Room 403, okay?"

Nearly everyone was on the bus now. The last students were at the front desk turning in their keys. Ms. Burella found Chuck Matson, the savvy young math teacher who had agreed to come along as head chaperone.

"Chuck, would you go up and take a look in Room 403?" Ms. Burella wasn't smiling anymore.

"What's up, Leslie?" Mr. Matson was not easily rattled.

"Just go take a look. See if everything looks in place." Leslie Burella was practically giving orders now.

Chuck Matson grabbed a key for Room 403 and dashed up the stairs. As he entered the hotel room, he made a quick scan of the room, looking and smelling for anything out of the ordinary. Even though Leslie Burella was vague, he figured this must have something to do with alcohol or drugs. Those are always the big issues on these trips.

He checked all the obvious places: under the beds, behind the furniture, even behind the shower curtain. He found a garbage can full of junk food wrappers, but that was about it.

"Leslie's working too hard," he thought as he headed for the door.

That's when he spotted the little refrigerator under the television. "Hey, my room didn't have one of those!"

Of course, in most hotels the refrigerator is well-stocked with a variety of items, mostly containing alcohol. But much to Mr. Matson's relief, he found that this one still had the plastic tie wrap from the hotel manager that shows at a glance nothing had been removed. He knew Leslie would be pleased at the news. Once again, he headed for the door.

Yet again, he paused, "I wonder?"

Chuck Matson walked back to the refrigerator and took another look at the tie wrap that secured the door shut. Sure enough, the plastic lock had been tampered with and seemingly cut, *melted* and then rejoined. At once looking inside, he did a quick inventory of the contents. "Bottles of wine, vodka, schnapps . . . well it seems that everything is here. But wait . . . water in the wine bottle?" Sure enough! Any bottle that provided the ability of disguise had been removed of its contents and refilled with water instead.

Chuck bolted down the stairs, slamming the door behind him to protect the scene of the crime. "Leslie! Who was in Room 403?"

He explained what he had found and they ravaged through Leslie's briefcase searching for the rooming list.

As the students impatiently waited on the idling charter bus, the four residents of Room 403, now prime suspects in the case, were asked to disembark. Leslie Burella would interrogate two of them, Chuck Matson would take on the others, one at a time, of course, to make sure their stories were consistent.

Mr. Matson would talk to Elana and Jen. (Mr. Matson had them both in his math class the previous year.) Elana would often come in on Monday morning talking about her "social calendar" from the previous weekend, but insisted that she had been clean from drugs and booze since ninth grade. "I just like to hang with my friends." Elana would say. "They can be stupid if they want—but it's not for me . . . not any more." It didn't help that Elana was frequently called into the dean's office at school, and it always seemed she was released for lack of evidence. Elana insisted her trouble was due to the clothing she wore, usually tie-dye shirts and jeans that always appeared dirty and frayed.

Jen, on the other hand, was a straight-A student headed for Yale, providing, of course, that her last semester of transcripts measured up in the final screening at the end of this term. She was another one who always hung around after the concert and helped Ms. Burella put away stage equipment. She had even stayed up once all night painting sets for the musical. To Mr. Matson, it seemed a waste of time to even question Jen, but to be consistent, he had to put her through the routine. The math teacher was pleased to hear her plea of innocence.

Meanwhile, Ms. Burella had to face Rachel and Michelle. She was shocked to find out that her leading virtuoso would have even been near a room with alcohol, and she was eager to prove her innocent. Rachel supplied all the right answers which enabled Ms. Burella to breathe a sigh of relief.

On the other hand, Michelle was by far the most defensive, which was typical of the attitude that she brought into the classroom on most school days. She was reluctant to answer any questions and muttered something about all the other people in the room last night. "What about the girls from Room 307?" she repeatedly asked. "Why don't you ask *them* who got drunk in Room 403?" Ms. Burella was certain that Michelle was guilty, but there was no confession in sight. Somebody was going to have to come forward with the truth, but so far there seemed to be no clear solution.

Leslie Burella and Chuck Matson met near the busload of restless students now consumed with rumors and anxiety. "Well, Chuck, what do you think? What's our next move?" Ms. Burella was preoccupied with anger and disbelief.

Just at that point, Rachel walked up and said, "I'm sorry, but I have a confession. I was there. I did it."

Matson and Burella stared at the star violinist in disbelief. "Rachel, you do know that drinking on tour is a 'go-home offense'?" Ms. Burella finally uttered.

Rachel stood silently, then finally said softly, "Yes . . . but I couldn't lie to you. I respect you too much."

Mr. Matson interjected, "Can you tell us who else was there, Rachel? We *need* to sort this thing out!"

Rachel was in tears. "Look, I'll turn myself in, but please don't tell me to rat on my friends!" She turned and walked away.

B. As a class, in small groups or in your personal journal consider these questions:

1. What do you do next? The orchestra is on the bus waiting to go to the festival, but you can't perform the Wieniawski without Rachel, and you've both conceded to the fact that she has committed a "go-home offense." Do you send her home and throw the competition, or do you bend the rules since "the show must go on?" What are the positive and negative ramifications of either decision? What are the issues concerning the setting of precedence when managing a group of students?

2. The urgency in this particular situation is perpetuated by the nature of the competitive event at hand. What is the value of such an event? What are the issues involved in designing the performance goals of your groups around competition?

3. What about the other students in the room? Did Rachel act alone? Should she be granted leniency for being the only one willing to confess? How will you send out the message that this sort of behavior will not be tolerated?

Development

A. Spend a few moments in small groups discussing the following questions (you may wish to assign one question to each group).

1. Is it part of the role of a music teacher to teach and

advocate values? Is it possible not to? Why or why not?

2. Create a list of the pros and cons of competitive festivals as related to school performance groups. Try to arrive at a conclusive statement that summarizes your philosophy regarding such events.

3. Make a short list of a few basic rules you think would be reasonable when traveling with a group of students.
What is it you wish to accomplish with the enforcement of these rules?

B. This case deals with the two issues of discipline and competition which frequently become entwined when dealing with performance ensembles. In discussing Ms. Burella's dilemma, we will discuss competition first.

As the old adage goes, "It doesn't matter whether you win or lose . . . until you lose." This in itself will become the battle cry for many a public school music director as they lead their musical teams on to the playing field. In fact, many will make this the very basis of their argument: "Music is not a matter of winning or losing, it's a matter of beauty!"

What is certain, however, is that the average person, regardless of culture and upbringing, can hardly ignore the motivational strength of a competitive event. It is among the very most fundamental principles of the capitalistic society in which we live. So it shouldn't be surprising that one of the most effective motivational tools in the classroom is to set a goal and challenge the students to surpass it. This in turn might cause the group to pull together with a spirit of teamwork that might not have otherwise been possible. It might also require a commitment on the part of the individual that would not have seemed worthy had the objective not been placed so high. Ms. Burella said it herself: "Give them something to work for so that they can accomplish it as a team! We are only as strong as the weakest member, so let's get to work!"

On the other hand, what about the students and directors that become more obsessed with the trophy case on the wall than the music being created in the rehearsal room? At what point do parents and administrators become addicted to competitive success, which ultimately evaluates your program by an accumulation of numerical charts and score sheets, instead of the intrinsic aesthetic value and beauty of the musical experience itself? Further complicate this with the certain subjectivity of any given adjudicator, and soon you are sending a mixed and confusing message to your students: "So, is music only meaningful if we win?"

While festival performance opportunities will vary by region and the ability of your group to travel, the following is an overview of the types of activities that are available to school performance ensembles.

Local and District Festivals

Usually organized by one or more teachers within the district itself, or perhaps even the music coordinator, these types of festivals will give groups an opportunity to perform for other groups similar to their own. They may or may not be adjudicated, but the greatest value is for your groups to hear other musicians their own age. It is important that you teach them how to listen and respond to what they have heard, or you will simply be perpetuating a competitive event without the ratings. When you return to the classroom, encourage your students to find something positive about the other groups, attributes they would want to bring to their own ensemble as well.

In rare instances, there are some districts that will in fact turn district festivals into competitive events in which not only the ensembles are evaluated but their directors as well. This will tell you a great deal about the role of music education and its meaning in that district.

Regional Festivals

Frequently organized and hosted by a specific school or university, or sometimes by the local chapters of the music teachers' and directors' associations. Like many district festivals, these events usually have a focus on the shared musical experience, sometimes with a clinician that will work with each ensemble following their performance presentation. If hosted by a college or university, there may be an appearance by the premier host ensemble to help encourage interest in the program of that institution. Once again, you will want to brief your students on what to listen for, particularly if the clinician takes time to work with the other ensembles in front of the audience. Let them know that there is much to learn from every performing group, regardless of whether they are perceived to be more or less advanced than your own.

State Adjudication/Rating Festivals

These festivals are usually organized by the state division of MENC, and largely conform to national standards set forth by the parent organization. These festivals claim to be competitive against a norm generally using a five-point scale including ratings such as superior, excellent, good, fair, and needs improvement. Some states will mandate a sight-reading component as well. In this model every participant can conceivably walk away with a superior rating, although it is more typical to see a fairly even distribution of ratings over the course of a two-day event. Even though efforts are made to make these "non-competitive" events, students will perceive the rating system as a *ranking* system and compare themselves to other groups at the festival in a competitive way.

Commercial Rating Festivals

Mostly sponsored by tour management organizations, the festival component of these events are much like the state adjudication type festivals. They may have a similar rating system, or they may have an award structure such as Gold, Silver, and Bronze Medals, or even trophies and plaques, but the fundamental principle is the same. All groups have the potential to return home with the highest possible rating. These festivals are usually held at a theme park or near a major tourist attraction and will be offered as part of a bigger package that includes hotels, buses, meals, and even airfare. They will have a tendency to vary in quality because the priority of the organizer is often that of a tour manager, not festival coordinator. Before buying such a package, you may want to request a list of other schools that have participated in the program and talk with other directors about the merits of the musical experience.

Commercial Competitive (Ranking) Festivals

Similar in management to the Commercial Rating Festivals mentioned above, these, too, will have "all inclusive package deals" for accommodations and travel arrangements. But the festival itself will be competitive in that there will only be one group to take first place or the sweepstakes award. They are usually divided into performance group categories so similar groups compete against each other for first, second, and third place in each section. Often the group with the highest score throughout the two- or three-day festival will be awarded an overall sweepstakes trophy, which may be exciting for the recipient, but will basically send all the other groups home feeling like second-class citizens. Here again, even though seemingly objective in structure, these festivals can vary a great deal in quality. In addition to checking out the references of other directors, find out who the adjudicators are and where they come from. This will help you determine the overall integrity of the musical components of the package.

Regional/State Competitive Events

Many states have competitive festivals as well, with a similar approach to scoring and awards, but without the flash tour packaging that accompanies the commercial events. These might be organized by the state directors association or even an individual school district or parent booster club. An excellent example are the numerous band reviews that take place throughout small town America every spring and fall. Bands will come by the busload to compete against one another in various events and categories, followed by an awards ceremony where the groups are ranked in numeric order according to their scores. Here again, there will be one group acknowledged for their outstanding achievement, and that will, in a sense, become the norm to judge all other groups. It is interesting to note that these type of events are often scored on a "points-taken-away" basis. That is, everyone starts with a perfect score, and every time something is not quite right (a flute player is out of step, the trumpets go out of tune), a point is taken away. The group with the most points left over will reign victorious. Some will say this advocates precise, but amusical performance as it is almost impossible to put a point value, negative or positive, on an aesthetic musical experience. Festivals of this nature exist for symphonic bands, orchestras, and choirs as well.

Your choice of festival and/or competitive events will depend on the priorities you have set for your program as well as those set by the district. If rank-based competition has been the norm, then it will take a number of years to instill more aesthetically-based values in your students. Conversely, you my find yourself simply searching for an activity that gives your students a tangible, motivational goal. In either case, the way that you prepare your students for such an experience, musically and mentally, will be crucial to the intrinsic musical value once the event draws to a close.

The difficulty in Leslie Burella's dilemma was that ultimately a large part of her self-perceived success came down to the behavior of one student. Placing such emphasis on a competitive event puts one in the position where they may choose to compromise ethical standards that they would otherwise consider unalterable.

If Leslie is to follow her own policy regarding a "go-home offense," then there is really nothing to discuss here. The student made a mistake; send her home. But having led the ensemble this far, what is Ms. Burella's obligation to the ensemble? And what about the other girls who apparently got away with it?

In creating policies for students traveling in school performance ensembles, you may want to consider the following:

1. Design and implement rules and regulations that are consistent with those of the school and/or the district in which you are teaching. Make sure you are standing behind the policies set forth by the administration, and likewise make sure they will stand behind you. When possible, include in the cost of your trip the expense of taking along an administrator to handle such a crisis should one occur. This will also help to preserve your role as a musician who is a dynamic and inspirational leader, as opposed to chief police officer.

2. Make sure the rules you make for your students are fair, yet enforceable. Once students get away with breaking a rule, and they go on seemingly unnoticed, your policies will begin to unravel from within.

3. Create an environment that encourages mutual respect. If it becomes a process of students vs. teachers and chaperones, the adults are apt to lose. Assume that your students will rise to the highest standards, but be quick to respond if they step out of line. It is simply human nature that most people will only aspire to the lowest common denominator. Your students will always be watching to see what is the very least you are willing to accept, not only with disciplinary issues, but with musical standards as well.

Improvisation

A. The buses sit idling in the parking lot loaded with students awaiting the festival events of the day. The time has come for you to tell them what you have found. Write out a brief statement that summarizes what has occurred and what you are going to do about it. Regardless of your decision about Rachel, your statement should include something that reiterates the meaning of your attendance at this festival in the first place.

B. Read your statement aloud to the rest of the class. Discuss how they differ from one another and how they reflect the priorities you have set for your program.

Recapitulation

A. In cooperative groups, take a moment to reflect on the national standards as set forth by MENC. Discuss how festivals and competitions coordinate and encourage success in these standards. Briefly sketch out a proposal for Ms. Burella's next tour which you might submit to the school board for approval. This should include the goals and objectives of taking such a trip, as well as a brief outline of the expectations of the participating students.

B. Share your proposal with the rest of the class.

In the Thicke of It!

Introduction

One of the most important tasks of an ensemble conductor is the selection of repertoire. For the band, orchestra, or chorus, the repertoire *is* the textbook. Studying and performing musical literature provides the mechanisms by which the conductor develops musical concepts, builds musical skills, increases technical proficiency, and teaches the connection of music to culture. By performing musical compositions in diverse styles and from various periods of history, the members of the ensemble gain insights into culture from a historical perspective. The playing and singing of music from different cultures enables students to learn something about others and themselves.

The literature and the repertoire which the ensemble studies and performs are reflective of the conductor's musical and educational goals. It may be trite, but the truth is that the adage "you are what you eat" becomes "you are what you perform."

In the following case, Dan Roberts is called to defend his repertoire choices as well as his ethics and values. Although he is the choral director, the situation could easily have happened to the conductor of an instrumental ensemble as well. The case deals with goals and objectives for a performing ensemble and the issue of sacred music in public schools. It also deals with the skills a teacher needs when dealing with parents to resolve conflict.

Exposition

A. Read the Case: *In the Thicke of It!*

As of December 13th, Daniel Roberts had been pleased with his accomplishments at Madison High School. Located in a middle-class suburban community, the Madison County Unified School District seems much more supportive of the arts than any other environment he has known from his own schooling. Even the principal, Anthony Seriglio, has taken an active interest in his vision for developing a diverse, yet comprehensive, choral music education program at the district's only high school.

In many ways, Madison High School is the pride of the district and the community alike. Since the arrival of the current principal seven years ago, the school has received important recognition in both academics and athletics. Last year, Madison High School was recognized as a "Distinguished Institution of Learning" by the State Board of Education, an organization that rewards schools which demonstrate outstanding student SAT scores. With a special declaration from the governor, this award constitutes additional funding for special programs and curriculum development. In addition, the basketball and football teams have both made the league playoffs for the past three years in a row. And this year the football team returned with the league championship for the first time in the history of the school. Perhaps the most impressive fact of all is that while the Madison campus is nearly two-thirds Caucasian, an innovative counseling "safety net" program has produced a dramatic increase in the extracurricular involvement as well as the academic success of the remaining third of the student body, composed primarily of African-American and Hispanic students.

The community largely credits Principal Seriglio for the success of the Madison High School students, but Mr. Seriglio in turn credits the parents and local businessmen who have come forward with time and money to make his dreams possible. The new computer lab and the flashy new football uniforms are both the result of an assertive parent group that convinced local industry of the importance of investing in education.

The development of a comprehensive arts program was clearly the next phase of growth in Mr. Seriglio's "distinguished" school. His decision to hire Daniel Roberts was risky given his lack of teaching experience, but Roberts's professors and student teaching supervisor raved about his boundless energy and his ability to motivate students. This seemed particularly crucial following the departure of Mrs. Dearborn, the previous choral director who participated in the "Golden Handshake" early retirement program. Mr. Seriglio suspects that Dorothy Dearborn was once a great music teacher, but she had long ago succumbed to the path of least resistance, producing virtually the same concert each season with an occasional tour *only* if the band director was willing to organize it.

Even still, the students loved her; therefore, finding a replacement for her became a delicate issue. Seriglio saw in Daniel Roberts the right balance of contagious enthusiasm and musical ability that would create a program worthy of the recognition bestowed on the rest of the school.

As the Winter Concert drew near, Mr. Seriglio and Mr. Roberts appeared to be well on their way to attaining their collective goals. The autumn months had been long and worrisome for Daniel, as his "vision" was frequently challenged by the students of Madison High School. Nobody had expected this year to go smoothly, especially not the seniors, who were certain they would never have another musical experience which would even come close to the big choral festival down in Orlando last spring.

But one by one, the members of the Madison High School Choir were beginning to understand what Mr. Roberts meant by "musical integrity." When the second movement of the Bernstein "Chichester Psalms" actually came together last Friday, everyone sensed a new energy that even the seniors had to admit was beyond anything they had experienced in their previous three years at Madison. Finally, the students were willing to admit that they could believe in the music, they could believe in the upcoming concert, and perhaps most importantly, they could believe in Mr. Roberts and his new style of leadership.

The dress rehearsal on Tuesday night provided the last vote of confidence for everyone. The Bernstein piece went together easily with the instrumentalists, and the singers seemed to be excited to have an opportunity to perform with local professional musicians. Likewise, the two Victoria motets worked especially well in the cavernous space of the auditorium. Concluding the program with Mendelssohn's "Heilig" for double chorus and Jester Hairston's rousing spiritual "Wonderful Counselor," Mr. Roberts was convinced that this perfect ending would surely offer something for everyone. And with the choir singing so well this early in the year, what a wonderful first impression this would make!

Because of the success of the previous night's rehearsal, Dan Roberts couldn't get to school soon enough on Wednesday morning. The only thing left to do before Thursday's concert was to put the final touches on his masterpiece and bask in the glory of a job well done. He was anxious to walk across campus and pick up his mail, hoping that someone might actually stop to ask, "How's it going?" to give him a window of opportunity to boast for a moment on what he knew would be a fabulous debut of the "new" Madison H.S. choral program! As he entered the front office, he caught Mr. Seriglio's eye as he hurried toward the conference room.

"You'd better check your box," said Mr. Seriglio, who was clearly distracted.

Mr. Roberts turned to Mr. Seriglio's secretary. "Is he angry at me or just dreading a meeting?"

"You'd better check your box," said Mrs. Anderson, who was known for her efficiency and directness.

Mr. Roberts felt his heart quicken as he turned to reach for the morning mail. There he found the following letter:

In the Thicke of It!

Citizens for Better Schools

15 December 1997

Mr. Anthony Seriglio, Principal
Madison High School
2324 Hamilton Street
New Hope, MA 03524

Dear Mr. Seriglio:

I am extremely concerned about what I am certain
will become a highly controversial issue on your campus.
Last night I sat through the last twenty minutes of the
dress rehearsal for Thursday's concert while waiting to
give my son a ride home. While I am pleased that the
students seem to like the new choral director, I was
appalled and affronted by the music they were singing,
as I am sure many others in our community will be as
well.

My first cause for alarm was an extensive work sung
in Hebrew. While I don't speak the language, it was
obvious to me that this was some kind of praise song,
and I found this to be extremely offensive in the
context of freedom in our public schools. As my preoccu-
pation with this issue continued to fester, I was further taken aback when the rehearsal concluded with a
piece the director referred to as an "African-American
spiritual." This was clearly musical propaganda with
heavy religious overtones, neither of which has a place
even in this extracurricular program. What are we
teaching our children?

Having discussed this issue with my wife, she, too,
is alarmed by this situation, not only on behalf of her
own son's involvement, but for all school children who
are being indoctrinated by inappropriate teaching
materials. She shares my desire for immediate action in

135

this situation, not just because of her position on the school board, but mostly as a concerned parent.

I recommend that you meet with the choral director at once, and advise him to reschedule or reprogram Thursday's concert. Doing so is likely to save you a great deal of contention, and perhaps even serious litigation.

Respectfully,

F. Cranius Thicke

F. Cranius Thicke
Citizens for Better Schools

The euphoria of just moments before had disintegrated into heartache. Mr. Roberts's mind was racing with confusion and anger. He walked out of the office past the closed door of the principal's office, even bypassing his ritualistic stop at the coffee machine. He would have no trouble keeping his adrenaline up this morning.

The general music classes of the morning passed slowly. It was difficult to keep his train of thought, let alone answer the student's questions. He had too many questions of his own to answer.

By third period on Wednesday, life was neither as simple or as gratifying as it was just a few hours earlier. And worst of all, Mr. Roberts had to face the choir in less than a one-half hour with not only a solution to his problem, but with a rationale to keep his dignity intact as well. He had finally won the confidence of his students, but now he wasn't even sure if he had confidence in himself.

B. In small cooperative groups, select a facilitator, recorder, encourager, summarizer, and reporter. Discuss one of the following questions:

1. Should the concert be canceled? Why or why not?
2. How should Mr. Roberts deal with the concern of Mr. Thicke? How can this become a win/win agreement?
3. What constitutes appropriate repertoire? What is the criteria for selecting such music?

Development

A. In your groups create a t-shirt logo (non-verbal representation) for your choir, orchestra, or band. Be able to explain how the logo reflects the values of the ensemble.

B. Choosing Repertoire

The music your ensembles play reflects your values as a musician and as an educator. Because ensembles rehearse their music over a significant period of time, often an entire semester, your selection is very important. For your ensembles, this selection is equivalent to their textbooks in other classes. For some students, it may be only serious music to which they are exposed. As in the case of Mr. Thicke, you may be called on to defend the music your students are performing.

In 1989 Stephen Covey wrote a very popular book titled *The 7 Habits of Highly Successful People*. He describes particular characteristics that are common in those who achieve at high levels. These principles can be applied to the selection of repertoire, and to the issue of Mr. Thicke's letter. When selecting repertoire it is important to remember the following:

1. Choose music for its inherent musical value. Do not be swayed by the "flavor of the month." Do not rely exclusively on music that arrives in the mail in a promotion kit from a particular publisher. Although that is one way to see what is new, and often there is some wonderful repertoire, it should not be the exclusive way you choose your repertoire. Adopt Covey's Habit One: be proactive.

Seek out repertoire from many sources. Collect programs from concert performances at conferences or at other schools. Peruse catalogues from the publishers. Check out music from the local college or university library as well.

2. Begin the process early. In chapter two, Covey writes, "Begin with the end in mind." Know where you are going. Select music with an overall plan in mind for the entire year. Perhaps you may wish to choose something from each of the historical periods. Or you may focus each concert around a particular theme. In any case, have a plan. All of your music should be selected by the beginning of the previous summer. Then you have the entire summer to study your scores while you provide the music retailer with enough time to order your selections to ensure delivery by September. If you are beginning a new job, seek out programs of concerts performed by your ensemble in the past. This will give you some good ideas.

3. When programming each concert, think of a three-part formula. The first piece should be what we call "in your face." It should open your concert by making a statement. It should cause the listeners to sit up and be engaged. The next section should "give them something to think about." The major work in a choral concert would fit here. For instrumental ensembles, perform a multi-movement work of some substance. Finally, "send them home smiling." Find a closing piece that ends each concert with the audience feeling satisfied.

Remember Covey's Habit Three: Put first things first. Check the national standards. What musical skills do you wish to teach? What music of other cultures do you wish to include? How will the music your ensemble performs connect to the world beyond your rehearsal? What preparation will your students need in order to render the repertoire you have chosen successfully? Sequence your ensemble goals for the year. What will you do first? For example, if you are performing a renaissance piece, what experiences might help the students get the style "into their ears?" If the piece is from the twentieth century, what issues must you address? In looking at specific pieces, check the ranges, tessitura, meter, text (if it is vocal), and accompaniment. Do you have the resources to perform the piece?

4. Covey writes in Habit Six about synergy, where his definition states "in relating [elements] to each other, they create bold new forms of each other that add even more to their value." Simply put, "the whole is greater than the sum of its parts." When choosing music for your performing groups, the concept of synergy is important. Remembering your goals, the repertoire serves as the framework for the overall values you teach. Synergy helps students make higher order connections and enhances their ability to critique and evaluate.

5. Covey's last point is to "sharpen the saw." From the perspective of your students, the repertoire you choose needs to stretch them in new directions. The music they sing or play needs to be challenging for them and challenging for you. Remember, that both of you will be living with these selections for a significant period of time. You, as the conductor, must feel that the music provides enough musical stimulation for you to sustain the interest of your students throughout the rehearsal period.

In dealing with Mr. Thicke, Covey says, "seek first to understand, then to be understood" (Habit Four), and "think win/win" (Habit Five). In the case of Cranius Thicke, he believes he is doing the right thing. In this country, parents do have a say in what their children learn in schools. Like any good parent, he wants what he believes is right for his child. Listen to what he *is* saying and to what he *is not* saying. In addition, you must know the children you are teaching. Who are they? Where do they come from? What are the political, religious, philosophical, social, and economic factors in the community where you teach? Remember, knowledge is power. If you have chosen your repertoire according to the guidelines outlined above, you will have something of substance upon which to present your case. Seek out the real issues. In negotiating a win/win solution, try to see the case from the other side. Then determine how much you are willing to compromise. Will you agree to have a committee of parents approve your repertoire selections? Will you agree to be more sensitive in the future to points of view that are different from yours? In other words, what are you willing to do that will not compromise your values while accommodating alternative viewpoints?

Improvisation

A. Review the MENC national standards for high school performing groups.

B. Develop a handbook for your ensemble. Include philosophy, goals, and objectives. Describe ensemble audition requirements and course expectations. Explain how you will assess the progress of your students.

Recapitulation

A. Exchange handbooks with your fellow students. Critique the handbooks and make suggestions for improvement.

B. In small groups, role-play the meeting between Seriglio, Roberts, and Thicke.

Marching to a Different Drummer

Introduction

Starting a new job always causes anxiety. Replacing an icon only increases that anxiety. Veteran music teachers will confirm that students always think that last year was better. They ask to perform the same repertoire even though they did not like it when they worked on it the previous year. As time passes the past always seems to get better. Being the new kid on the block, whether it is your first job or not, is difficult. Where to begin and finding out what the students already know are the easy things. What is difficult is winning over the loyalties of students who loved their former teacher. In a sense, the program is not yours until all of the students of the previous teacher have graduated or moved on. Achieving success that first year will take all of the interpersonal intelligence you have.

Meet Jerry McAllister. As an alumnus of Morales High School, he thought that he might bypass some of the indignities of developing his own following. Ultimately, however, it came down to one crucial event in which his students would come to find out what Mr. McAlllister was really all about.

Exposition

A. Read the Case: *Marching to a Different Drummer*

Jerry McAllister knew the first couple of years at Morales High School would be a rough go, but enough is enough! The fight out on the marching field last night was the last straw. Could it be worth all this?

Strangely enough, Jerry was a Morales alumnus. He was an all-star student in the music department, and then he went away to music school on a full scholarship. After a year working in a middle school in North Carolina, the principal at Morales was delighted to lure him back home following the retirement of the beloved William Robbins. Robbins had been the band director at Morales for thirty-eight years, known as the local music man to over two generations in this small southeastern town. Even the current principal had Mr. Robbins for ninth-grade band.

In fact, nearly every musical event and tradition in the Morales Valley seemed to have some link to Robbins's guidance and influence over the past four decades. It was his idea to begin the fall band review, which had become an annual weekend of festive activities that local commerce had come to applaud. Likewise, his Band Jamboree in the spring was an important alumni event for anyone in town who had grown up in the Morales school district music program. Robbins had begun the music boosters organization, which in turn led to annual tours that had brought the band and the community notoriety throughout the eastern United States and beyond. At the very least, Robbins was a town hero.

But Jerry McAllister was cut from the same cloth. His earliest musical experiences were under Robbins's baton, so surely if there was anyone able to keep up the tradition, McAllister was the one.

Things might have gone more smoothly if McAllister hadn't left the valley for a few years. While in college, he was challenged to reexamine everything he knew about music and especially teaching. At first it was difficult as he actually found himself becoming defensive about the way he himself had been taught, but over time he began to form new ideals and approaches that he knew could only enrich the lives and talents of his students. The year at the middle school only solidified those beliefs, as he was forced to establish his identity as a teacher. Now he was going home. New energy, new ideas, new approaches, and an environment where he was known and accepted. This should be a snap!

After a brief "honeymoon" period, things began to unravel. The very first issue was with the marching band. McAllister was ready to bring them up to the best and latest drill routines, but the band had grown accustomed to a more "traditional" marching routine that had arrived with Bill Robbins nearly forty years ago. "How can you walk on tradition, Mr. McAllister? After all, you went here yourself!" Parents and students alike were critical of change.

From there, the issues became more complex. There were arguments with the boosters about the allocation of funds, the purchase of instruments, and huge expenditures for extravagant tours that had little to do with music or education.

This year, his third, was critical. This was Jerry's tenure year. If he had a successful year, he would be set for life. In fact, Jerry McAllister was thinking things should be smoothing out, and seemingly they had been doing just that. Each year there had been a bigger contingency of students and parents who could appreciate his style of leadership and his approach to education, yet there were still a few hold-outs. Among these, trumpet player Mikey Fischer had been the most vehement. In fact, when Mikey came out for marching band at the beginning of the year, Mr. McAllister made him sign a contract regarding expectations for attendance and conduct, both of which had been areas of contention over the past two years. But all in all, Jerry McAllister had come to accept the hassles from the other Mikey Fischer types, while setting his sights on simply making it from one day to the next. That is, until the scene during marching practice last night.

"FISCHER! FALL OUT AND GET YOURSELF OVER

HERE!" McAllister belted across the practice field without the need of a megaphone. Mikey Fischer was at it again. Even students that usually laughed at his gags were starting to get annoyed at his ability to upstage the drum major and distract the band.

Mikey Fischer came to attention, but he didn't leave the field. He smirked as he laughed under his breath.

"FISCHER!" McAllister barked again. "Get over here!"

"Sorry, chief, I'm kinda busy!" Mikey shot back. It was a hung jury on the field. Some of the band laughed, others looked irritated.

That was it. Jerry McAllister took to the field and made a straight line through the formation to Mikey Fischer. Once there he looked him in the eye and quietly ordered, "Go home."

"What?" This was clearly not the reaction Mikey had expected.

"I said, go home! You're done." McAllister was calm but direct.

"I don't have to! This is my band and I'm stayin'." Mikey glanced around to take an inventory of his support.

"Go home!" McAllister was less calm now, but spoke more softly.

It was probably only ten or fifteen seconds, but anyone who was there will tell you it seemed like two hours until Mikey finally left the field, slammed the gate, and left the stadium with tires squealing in the distance.

The rest of the practice went like clockwork. No one dared to step out of line. Finally, after the last drill, it seemed that every student needed to share their opinion with Mr. McAllister.

"You did the right thing, Mr. McAllister."

"Don't you think you were kind of hard on him, Mr. M?"

"Mr. McAllister, what's gonna happen to him?"

In Jerry McAllister's mind, there was only one answer to the final and most pressing question. It was time to tell Mikey Fischer to drop out of band, not just because of last night, but as a result of two years of fighting with Mikey and the attitude that he represented. Except for one thing: Mikey Fischer was the principal's son.

B. What do you think? Share your thoughts with a partner or with your class.

1. Did Jerry McAllister make the right decision when he threw Mikey out of band? Should he have handled things differently? Is it significant that Mikey's father was the school principal? How will this affect his tenure review?

2. What do you think happened next? What are some possible scenarios? What is the most proactive approach Jerry McAllister can take to keep the program moving forward?

3. What are the considerations when taking over a well-established music program? What components will be in place and which ones will need to be rebuilt? What are the advantages and disadvantages of accepting a program where your predecessor has had a long and successful career?

Development

A. On a separate piece of paper, draw a picture or representation of a cohesive music program. Be sure to include characters that depict the role of the teacher and his or her role within such an organization.

B. Some music teachers are able to identify precisely when, sometimes even to the day of the specific event, they were able to assume full ownership of the music program of which they had been given charge. For a fortunate few, it may only take a few weeks, but for many the controversy may continue for years. Maintaining one's self-esteem and dignity during those early years may be challenging, but those who survive will usually tell you, it's worth the wait.

Even those who study early childhood psychology recognize that it is simply human nature to test the limits. From the time we are infants throughout adulthood, we go about life looking for the threshold of acceptability given the unspoken social etiquette of any given environment. So it should be no wonder that students of any age will go through the same process. In addition, as stated in the introduction, memory will perpetuate the accomplishments of the past with much more glamour than ever existed in the first place. If in fact the past includes events of exceptional achievements, then the young teacher has an even greater challenge ahead.

An earlier case discussed the importance of settings goals in order to achieve success. This is crucial when entering a situation where many around you will have goals they have adopted for you on your behalf. It is important at this point to walk the fine line between honoring tradition and working to establish that which is uniquely your own. Even when assuming a teaching position where the quality of instruction before your arrival was of lesser quality, the students and parents may not have recognized the deficiencies. If the previous person had at very least created an affirming atmosphere, students will expect you to employ similar projects to do the same, unable to differentiate what is process and what is personality.

The dilemma is clear; the solution is not. Is it better to make the fundamental changes to a program in the first year to get progress more rapidly under way? Or is it better to test the waters for a year and go with what is already in place? While philosophical change may be taking place underneath, it is usually wise to avoid major change in the first year until there has been time to truly evaluate which issues are of crucial significance and which issues simply become a vehicle for a power struggle.

There will be a few key people that will become important resources during the period of transition. Finding a mentor, either at the same school site or elsewhere in the district, is imperative. Whether this person is a music teacher or not is less important than whether they have an empathy for what you are going through. Choose someone who has had to follow a dynamic leader. Even if this person is unable to offer concrete solutions to specific problems, having the support of someone who understands the frustrations at hand becomes a stabilizing force.

Similarly, there will be parents and students that are more progressive than others and will welcome new energy and ideas. The ability to identify these people and their role within the program is a two-fold process. There will be some who welcome change due to a conflict with the previous teacher. You may become a vehicle of their vindication when your intentions are simply to lend a compassionate ear. Pay attention to who is connected to whom in both the classroom and with the parents. Take a step back and ask, "Who do other students look up to, and why?" At that point, you can decide who is worth fighting for, and who will eventually graduate out of the program.

Confrontations like the one Jerry McAllister had with Mikey Fischer are very real. Whether Mikey knows it or not, he has appointed himself the chair of a committee to find out if Mr. McAllister really stands behind what he says. More importantly, the interaction took place in front of the entire band where everyone else was just as interested in the outcome as Mikey Fischer. At first, Mr. McAllister will feel his decisions are extremely unpopular, but if he has been clear in his goals and expectations, the students can only respect him for being true to his word.

A rule of thumb in such situations as this is to choose your battles carefully. Decide which issues are of lasting importance to your long-range goals, and which are simply short-term power struggles that will have little consequence if left to work themselves out. It may be worth compromising on the smaller issues in order to create more leverage for the crucial ones.

Occasionally it will be necessary to sit down and work out a compromise with a student. If the meeting is a result of a confrontation and the student is likely to still be carrying anger and resentment, a bit of careful planning can keep a potentially productive encounter from turning into an out-of-control nightmare. The student may not be seeking solutions, but simply looking for an opportunity to vent, in which case reason and logic will be of little use regardless of the teacher's position on the issue. If such a scenario is anticipated, have the student set up an appointment with a guidance counselor or department chair. It should be someone with authority but who has no particular stake in the matter at hand. This objective third party should be willing to serve as a facilitator, recapping the important points made on both sides and making sure each person has ample opportunity to speak. This will keep emotions at bay and eliminate comments that are usually better left unsaid. At the end, the facilitator can summarize what has been said and identify the common ground, or at least a viable compromise if there is any to be had.

The good news is, a confrontation such as the one with Mikey Fischer, if handled with appropriate fairness and great diplomacy, will often mark the turning point of a program. A few more students may feel a need to walk out in support of Mikey, but particularly when those that are left are invited to speak out or forever hold their peace, then a new era is set to begin.

This is also true in dealing with parent booster organizations, although an even greater level of diplomacy may be in order. Even school administrators seem to know which parents they can afford to offend, and which they cannot. An angry parent at a school board meeting can leave a path of destruction regardless of the validity of their cause. In addition to a mentor in the school community, it is helpful to have an administrator that you know will stand behind your decisions. If they will *not*, you must give careful consideration to what lies ahead and the ramifications therein. Keep in mind that for the first couple of years, administrators will be examining your thresholds and boundaries as well, and only over time will you be able to develop the kind of intuitive relationship that such delicate matters often require.

Some teachers simply refuse to work with parent booster clubs as they see it as more of a struggle than it's worth. Like the students in the classroom who you identify as allies, you will want to see parents who embrace your vision for long-term success in the pivotal positions of the organization. It may take a number of years to accomplish this, but the value of a group of parent advocates working for your collective cause cannot be underestimated. If a parent group is firmly in place when inheriting the program, it is useful to meet with the members of the organization one at a time. Use them as a resource to find out what has gone on before. Value their ideas and suggestions, but don't commit to anything you consider to be unfeasible or impossible. Meeting one-on-one will increase the likelihood that they will hear what you have to say and present an opportunity for a more frank and honest discussion.

For all of the above, integrity is the bottom line. It is tempting to tell people what they want to hear, particularly when it comes to aligning one group of people against another. It is also extremely dangerous. Once you have spoken unfavorably about another person, one has no way of knowing if you will speak unfavorably about them, too.

One way to align parents for your future success is to develop a sub-committee to deal with one of your long-range goals. Perhaps it will be a plan for a tour, or a recording project, or the band review you would like to host two years from now. A subcommittee can work at their own pace while maintaining a liaison to the main booster organization. This will give the new teacher an opportunity to handpick parents that best represent the persona of the future. If it is a long-term project, once it has come to fruition, you are likely to have recruiting leadership that is willing to step up to the next level of responsibility.

Such long-term projects will be useful in the classroom as well, particularly in targeting the younger students who will be in the program for an extended period of time. It is the enthusiasm of these underclassmen that will be vital for the recruitment process for the coming years. If they are excited about what the future might hold, they can't help but share it with their friends.

Is it more difficult to build a program from the ground up, or to assume leadership in a program that is already established and turn it around? It depends on who you are and what it is you wish to accomplish. Ultimately, however, those with clear goals and a strong sense of perseverance are the ones that survive. Most music teachers spend their entire careers developing interpersonal skills and diplomacy, but only those who are determined to succeed and have a clear definition of what it means to do so will remain.

Improvisation

A. Write a handbook for your band, orchestra, or choir. Make sure to include a "code of conduct" along with any other information regarding goals, objectives, and assessment procedures that would help you feel confident when dealing with a student like Mikey Fischer.

B. Design a logo for the cover of your handbook. Select a mascot and a t-shirt design for your ensemble.

Recapitulation

A. Swap handbooks and designs. Critique each by revising, adjusting, and editing as necessary.

B. Use desktop publishing to publish your handbooks.

The Right Choice

Introduction

Musical auditions are always an involved process. The callbacks, the monologues, and the casting present challenges for those who make decisions. It is always a relief when the cast list is finally posted. Unfortunately, some students will not "make the list." This is difficult for music teachers who believe that schools should provide opportunities for all the students who wish to participate.

Eric Jackson, the music teacher at Buchanan High School, believed just that. Mr. Jackson believed in Zoltán Kodály's philosophy that music and music programs should be accessible to all; however, the school musical was a different situation. Should the best person get the part or should the best part be a reward for the person who worked the hardest? This is the dilemma that Mr. Jackson must face in this case.

Exposition

A. Consider the issues in the Case: *The Right Choice*

Eric Jackson inherited the musical project from his predecessor at Buchanan High School. For twenty-five years the school had a reputation for excellence in theatrical productions.

The whole town rallied around the annual school musical. Curiously, people who would not attend the plays or the band concerts would not dream of missing the musical.

Mr. Jackson enjoyed doing the school musical each year. He was particularly looking forward to this year because he had a "great bunch of kids." They worked hard and were fun to teach. The musical served as their reward for the dedication they showed working on the traditional repertoire of the choral concert season.

Mr. Jackson was particularly lucky to have Erin Lewis in the choir. Erin was a straight-A student and had always been a mainstay in the alto section of both the Concert Choir and Madrigal Singers. This past year she was selected for the jazz choir. This was a most prestigious honor. Erin was no stranger to competition. In the classroom, on the stage, or on the athletic field, she was a fierce competitor. Jackson truly depended on her. And although Mr. Jackson never pre-cast his shows, he did have Erin in mind when he chose My Fair Lady for this year's production.

It was ten minutes to five on Friday afternoon and callbacks were nearly completed. There was one more set of boys to read for the role of Freddy. The parts of Higgins, Alfred P. Doolittle, and Pickering were firm. And although Mr. Jackson was not feeling ecstatic about Erin Lewis, he felt that she would do a very credible job in the leading role of Eliza Doolittle. In fact, Mr. Jackson had pretty much made up his mind when he looked up from his clipboard to see a new student standing in front of him. "May I help you?" Mr. Jackson asked.

"My name is Sondra Anderson and I would like to audition." Mr. Jackson thought for a moment and then decided, why not? After all, he really did not want to turn anyone away and did believe that everyone should have a chance. Although he had never met Sondra, he thought that perhaps this might be an opportunity to recruit another student for the choir.

"What part do you wish to audition for?" asked Mr. Jackson.

"I'd like to read for Eliza Doolittle," Sondra said.

"Very well," replied Mr. Jackson and he handed her the

scene where Eliza enters Higgin's house for the first time to ask for diction lessons. As soon as Sondra began to read, it became clear to everyone in the room, including Eric Jackson, that he had found his Eliza. She was perfect. When she sang, her voice was glorious. Just the right sound for Eliza as well. When she read with Nelson, Mr. Jackson's choice for Higgins, there was magic.

It was 5:30 p.m. and everyone had gone home when Eric Jackson returned to his office. As he began to type the cast list, he stopped when he came to the name Eliza Doolittle. What should he do? Sondra was clearly the best choice; yet Erin was a senior and had worked so hard for the choir. In addition, she was not all that bad. Erin was also a sure thing, and Mr. Jackson knew that if he gave her the part, she would work hard. On the other hand, Mr. Jackson did not know Sondra at all. Yet she was wonderful. What about the other students in the show? Did they deserve to have the best show possible? Still, could he do this to Erin? Finally, Mr. Jackson made his decision and posted the list.

As was his habit, Mr. Jackson held an "open door day" after each round of auditions. During this day, he would invite his students to sit down in his office one at a time and discuss their audition. In this case, by the time musical callbacks were over, everyone had a pretty good sense of how the show was going to look. Of course, the big problem with My Fair Lady is that there can only be one Eliza, but given tonight's turn of events, it seemed pretty cut and dry who that would be as well. Surely, even the other cast members would have seen the handwriting on the wall.

Monday was the day of reconciliation as students settled into their roles. By lunchtime, "open door day" was going fairly well. Tom was disappointed not to get "the Professor," but was relieved that he would not have to quit the baseball team to do the show. Jenny came in every year to find out what she could do better, but she seemed to be accepting her limitations as an actress. Students respected Mr. Jackson and the decisions he made, and once the initial disappointment wore off they were usually able to handle the truth.

Eric Jackson took a moment between students to sign some check requests, leave a quick phone message, and check his e-mail. As he looked up from the computer, there was Erin Lewis standing in the doorway.

"Hi, Erin," Mr. Jackson said. "Would you like to talk?"

"Sure." Erin sat down.

Mr. Jackson opened with his standard line, "What can I tell you about your audition, Erin?"

Erin burst into tears. "It's not fair! How could you do that!"

Mr. Jackson bolted upright in his chair and reached for the tissues. "Whoa! Wait a minute. What's goin' on?" This was not the rational Erin he knew.

"Well, it's my own fault!" she struggled out through the tears. "I should have known that's how it would turn out! You've never liked me and everybody knows that's what this program is about."

Mr. Jackson slumped back into his chair feeling bewildered and betrayed. Speaking at this point could only make the situation worse. Instead he chose to sit for a moment as she continued to sob. Finally she began to regain her composure. "It was obvious back in tenth grade how you choose soloists. Remember when Cathy Jacobs got that solo in Madrigal Singers?"

Eric Jackson scanned his memory trying to recall the solo, Cathy, and the audition. Oh yes, he could remember. Why is that coming up now, he wondered? "Go on," he prodded under his breath.

"You know who you're going to choose before you ever start these things." She was crying more now. "It has nothing to do with ability! Just because someone tells you what you want to hear, you give them what they want. And look at everything I've done for you over the years! Doesn't that matter?"

"Of course it matters! Take it easy for a . . . " Mr. Jackson tried to come to his own defense.

"No Mr. Jackson, *you* take it easy! I'm not willing to play these games anymore, so you can just have your musical and your choirs. I'm through!"

"Do you really feel that way, Erin?" Jackson was visibly hurt. She just sat sobbing while reaching for another tissue. "May I ask why you didn't come forward two years ago when Cathy got that solo? I had no idea that was even important to you."

"It wasn't! Well, it was! I didn't know then! Oh . . . you just don't understand!" She grabbed a tissue, stood up, and walked out the door.

B. Discussion

Do you agree with Mr. Jackson's decision? Which is more important to you, talent or merit? How far should one go in the name of quality? Is the play greater than the players? What do you think? Share your thoughts with the class.

Development

A. The following is a scene from *My Fair Lady*. Choose readers from within the class and perform the scene.

(HIGGINS comes down to the tea table. He looks at ELIZA quizzically; while deciding on a method of attack he pours himself some tea. He decides on restraint.)

HIGGINS: Well, Eliza, you've had a bit of your own back, as you call it. Have you had enough? And are you going to be reasonable? Or do you want any more?

ELIZA: You want me back only to pick up your slippers and put up with your tempers and fetch and carry for you.

HIGGINS: I haven't said I wanted you back at all.

ELIZA: *(turns to him)*: Oh, indeed. Then what are we talking about?

HIGGINS: About you, not about me. If you come back I shall treat you just as I have always treated you. I can't change my nature; and I don't intend to change my manners. My manners are exactly the same as Colonel Pickering's.

ELIZA: Oh, I see. (*She rises composedly and walks away.*) The same to everybody.

HIGGINS: Just so. (*He sits at the table.*)...The real secret, Eliza, is not having bad manners or good manners or any other particular sort of manners, but having the same manner for all human souls. The question is not whether I treat you rudely, but whether you ever heard me treat anyone else better.

ELIZA: (*with sudden sincerity*): I don't care how you treat me. I don't mind your swearing at me. I shouldn't mind a black eye; I've had one before this. But I won't be passed over.

HIGGINS: Then get out of my way, for I won't stop for you. You talk about me as if I were a motor bus.

ELIZA: So you are a motor bus: all bounce and go, and no consideration for anyone. But I can get along without you. Don't think I can't.

HIGGINS: I know you can. I told you you could. (*Pause, seriously*) You never wondered, I suppose, whether I could get along without you.

ELIZA: Don't try to get around me. You'll have to.

HIGGINS: (*arrogantly*): And so I can. Without you or any soul on earth. (*With sudden humility*) But I shall miss you, Eliza. I've learned something from your idiotic notions. I confess that humbly and gratefully.

ELIZA: Well, you have my voice on your gramophone. When you feel lonely without me you can turn it on. It's got no feelings to hurt.

HIGGINS: I can't turn your soul on.

ELIZA: Oh, you are a devil. You can twist the heart in a girl as easily as some can twist her arms to hurt her. What am I to come back for?

HIGGINS: (heartily): For the fun of it. That's why I took you on.

ELIZA: And you may throw me out tomorrow if I don't do everything you want me to?

HIGGINS: Yes, and you may walk out tomorrow if I don't do everything you want me to.

ELIZA: And live with my father?

HIGGINS: Yes, or sell flowers. Or would you rather marry Pickering?

ELIZA: (fiercely): I won't marry you if you asked me and you're nearer my age than what he is.

HIGGINS: (correcting her gently): Than he is.

ELIZA: (losing her temper and walking away from him): I'll talk as I like. You're not my teacher now. That's not what I want and don't you think it. I've always had chaps enough wanting me that way. Freddy Hill writes to me twice and three times a day, sheets and sheets.

HIGGINS: (coming to her): Oh, in short, you want me to be as infatuated about you as he is. Is that it?

ELIZA: (facing him, much troubled): No, I don't. That's not the sort of feeling I want from you. I want a little kindness. I know I'm a common ignorant girl, and you a book-learned gentleman; but I'm not dirt under your feet. What I done—(Correcting herself) What I did was not for the dresses and the taxis. I

157

did it because we were pleasant together and I come—came to care for you; not to want you to make love to me, and not forgetting the difference between us, but more friendly like.

HIGGINS: Yes, of course. That's just how I feel. And how Pickering feels. Eliza, you're a fool.

ELIZA: That's not a proper answer to give me.

HIGGINS: It's all you'll get until you stop being a plain idiot. If you're going to be a lady you'll have to stop feeling neglected if the men you know don't spend half their time sniveling over you and the other half giving you black eyes. You find me cold, unfeeling, selfish, don't you? Very well. Be off with you to the sort of people you like. Marry some sentimental hog or other with lots of money and a thick pair of lips to kiss you with and a thick pair of boots to kick you with. If you can't appreciate what you've got, you'd better get what you can appreciate.

ELIZA: (*desperate*): I can't talk to you; you turn everything against me. I'm always in the wrong. But don't you be too sure that you have me under your feet to be trampled on and talked down.

B. The audition is one component of the music program for which there is never enough time or diplomacy. After spending a great deal of time and energy building up a program of students who are enthusiastic and eager to test their wings, many of these same students will now be told in one way or another that they have reached their limitations and cannot go on. With this in mind, it is worth taking extra time to create a process that is both efficient and fair in an attempt to give every student an opportunity to "perform" to the best of his or her abilities.

The waters are further complicated because adolescence is a

time of exploration in every sense of the word. It is during these years that teens find those elements that define their personalities and that which they will contribute to society as a whole. For a fortunate few, they will recognize their strengths early on and emerge as young adults with goals and ambitions and a vision of "how they fit in." For a vast majority, however, they will rely on a specific individual to recognize this potential within them and draw these attributes out. As a music teacher, you are often bestowed with this responsibility of finding these "diamonds in the rough" and pulling them into the open.

This is particularly challenging for the ensemble director (which includes the director of a theater production) because you also have responsibilities to the ensemble as a whole and to the material you are performing. Which comes first? Do you choose the student who has worked the hardest or the one that will do the best job musically? There is no right answer. This is a decision that you must resolve for yourself.

What many teachers fail to see is that our students have their own dreams, their own insecurities, and their own thresholds for disappointment. So often we find ourselves playing the role of counselor, parent, psychologist, some or all of which we may be ill-prepared to do; in addition, it is often inappropriate that we would do so in the first place.

In the final analysis, a teacher must take a moment to trace a student's growth and development through the three or four years he or she participates in a comprehensive music program. Inherent in this process are questions like: What am I doing to challenge this student as he or she progresses from one year to the next? What opportunities are there within the program that allow for individual talents and abilities? What can I do to promote an environment that lets every student feel like an integral part of the ensemble? What do they bring to the team besides their musicianship? Many school districts have set up exploratory programs at the middle school level which will allow a student to take a music class for a period as short as six or eight weeks, simply to have the exposure to the arts and "test the water." As the student body progresses towards high school graduation, students will make choices. Some will focus their energies on getting into Harvard or Stanford. Some will begin building their position for "best senior athlete," and some will choose music. The point is that as students find direction in their lives, some attrition in the music program is bound to occur. Our goal as music teachers is to see that the attrition occurs as a result of the student feeling they've had a choice, as opposed to a process of elimination that has forced them out of our programs.

The following list of strategies will help promote equality and fairness among your students and thereby create an atmosphere that will allow them to feel they each have ample opportunities to succeed.

1. "Open Door Day." Consider some process which will allow each student to discuss what has taken place and what influenced your decision. While it is important to be gentle and sensitive, it is also important to be honest. If possible, counter the constructive criticism with acknowledgment of strengths of how they contribute to the program, while at the same time being careful not to come across as patronizing. A student will see right through that, and you may never be able to regain that credibility, once lost. Be careful not to make promises like, "if you only do this, you're sure to get in next time." This is almost certain to come back and haunt you.

2. Plan a program or choose a musical with rehearsals that emphasize the ensemble experience. Whether you are producing a musical or working with a one-hundred-member performance ensemble, always be aware that the real strength of your program comes from the shared satisfaction of the masses. If only from a political standpoint, you must realize that catering to three or four unusually talented students will fail to elicit the support of the parents, friends, and family of the greater ensemble. Include exercises that will allow the group to get to know one another

as people, not just musicians. Centering and focusing exercises that emphasize the power of the collaborative effort will tell every last person that the show can't go on without them.

3. Particularly at the secondary level, you will develop friendships with particular students who tend to spend a lot of time in the music building. Don't let such friendships take the place of social contacts that you would normally maintain with other adults. You can go for months without having a conversation with another teacher on campus if you don't force yourself to get out onto campus once in awhile and interact with your colleagues. This in turn will let students know you are not the only resource for their social lives and will keep relationships in a more healthy balance.

4. When you have student assistants to help with daily routine tasks, have clearly written guidelines about what is expected in their work, and what will happen if the work doesn't get done. Spend a moment to discuss these guidelines at the beginning of the semester and stick to what you have said. Otherwise, your prep period may become a study hall or even a social gathering place for students that have a free class period and nothing better to do. Allowing such arrangements to take place will often contribute to what other students perceive as favoritism.

5. Notice when your students do something right. Drop in on the soccer game. Go to the speech debate. Value the other activities that are important in your students' lives. Make sure you take a moment to mention the success of those studens the next time you see them. If it's noteworthy, acknowledge them in front of the rest of the ensemble.

6. Notice when your students do something wrong. Sometimes it seems easier just to let some things go, but

when you do, you are sending a non-verbal message that you are willing to accept less than the status quo. There will be instances when a student will venture out with an intentional mistake or infraction just to see if you care enough to act upon it. And remember, others are watching as well. Your ability to be consistent will be crucial when your integrity is on the line.

7. To be sure, there will be students that you get to know better and through their personal interests and self-motivation make themselves invaluable to your program. There may be occasions where you have to sit down and remind them of their role as a student and clearly define what you are willing to accept. Can they work at your desk? Can they use your phone for personal calls? Are they held responsible for the same policies as everyone else in the department? Once an exception has been made, it will be very difficult to justify your decision to a student who has been perhaps less "helpful" but is just as deserving.

In fact, consistency may be the most important single factor of an effective program administrator, which, as a music teacher, you are. Have your policies well-defined in your own mind and put them in writing. As a leader, your students, their parents and the community will look to you not only for your musicianship but also for your personal integrity and your ability to deal with people.

Improvisation

A. As a musician, reflect on your successes which have brought you here thus far. Have your landmark achievements been strictly a result of innate talent, or "rewards" for your willingness to work hard and get it right? Share an example of a previous teacher that selected you for an important role or position.

Try to identify why you were selected and what considerations that teacher must have had in making his or her decision.

B. Remember a time when you did not get a part, or a solo, or a spot on the team, or a seat in the ensemble that you wanted. Write yourself a letter from that teacher or conductor or coach explaining the decision.

Recapitulation

A. Share your letter with a friend in your class.

B. Watch the opening scene from the movie A *Chorus Line*. Then fast forward and watch the song "Nothing." Discuss your reactions with a friend or with your class.

Copyright or Copywrong

Introduction

Experienced music teachers all know someone who has broken the copyright laws. It is so common that many teachers don't really think too much about it. They need the material for their students and somehow this justifies breaking the law. Further, copy machines are everywhere. With the popularity and accessibility of the internet, issues of copyright become complicated. However, the fact of the matter is that much of the copying done in the name of education is against the law.

Music teacher Jason Andrew has a more serious problem than just needing an extra part or two copied. How he resolves it is important because he could jeopardize himself, his school, and the students. Andrew is, like all teachers, a role model. If he breaks the law, he will be sending a message to his students that he may not intend. What should Mr. Andrew do? What would you do in his situation?

Exposition

A. Read the Case: *Copyright or Copywrong*
Jason Andrew is the band director at Academy High School.

In the past five years of teaching there, Mr. Andrew has turned the marching band into champions. Last year, they moved from a Division B band (under 100 players) to a first-prize Division A ensemble with 125 playing musicians and a color guard of 40. His drum majors took highest honors at the state finals. Mr. Andrew was proud and the headmaster was proud, too. In fact, the Academy Marching Band was the pride of Canobie, New Hampshire—a small New England town just north of Boston.

Each May, as was his custom, Mr. Andrew met with the drill designer, color guard coach, and percussion instructor to plan the show for the following season. This year, they all wanted to do something special for the band. "Instead of using commercial arrangements," Mr. Andrew said, "let's do an original suite from the movie musical, *In Your Dreams.*" What a great idea, they thought. *In Your Dreams* had been popular some years back. The composer won an Academy award for best film score that year, and everyone knew and loved the songs.

Over the summer Mr. Andrew purchased a book of musical selections from *In Your Dreams.* He called the American Society of Composers, Authors, and Publishers (ASCAP) to locate the owner of the copyright and was told that it was Laurence Brothers Music. From the internet he downloaded the "permission to arrange" forms, filled them out, and sent them in. In the meantime, he began to work on the arrangement.

By the beginning of August, Mr. Andrew finished the arrangement and sent it to the drill designer. Just before band camp, everything was completed. He made several phone calls to Laurence Brothers regarding the permission, and he was promised by the folks there that a decision would be imminent. Band camp began the end of August. Confident that there would be no problem with the copyright permission, Mr. Andrew duplicated the parts and the staff began to teach the music and the drill routine to the band. In fact, after the band read through *In Your Dreams* for the first time, they put down their instruments and gave Mr. Andrew a standing ovation. This arrangement was sure to put the band over the top.

School opened after Labor Day and the band rehearsed intensely, practicing their show three afternoons each week and all day on Saturdays. The first competition was on Saturday, October 1st. The students worked hard because the arrangement was challenging. They did not want to disappoint Mr. Andrew.

Just to be on the safe side, Mr. Andrew made several calls to the permissions department at Laurence Brothers and was assured that an answer would be forthcoming. On Friday, September 30th, the day before the competition, Jason Andrew received the following fax:

Laurence Brothers Music

Dear Mr. Andrew:

We regret to inform you that permission to arrange *In Your Dreams* for marching band has been denied. A commercially available arrange-ment is scheduled for publication this year. We feel that our arrangement will suit your needs.

Sincerely,

Monica Strict

Monica Strict, Vice-President,
Copyrights and Permissions
Laurence Brothers Publications

Four-letter words raced through Mr. Andrew's head. What should he do? Should he scratch the band from the competition tomorrow? What about the rest of the season? Now he had no music and no marching band show. He looked for the Headmaster, but he was at a conference out of state. This deci-sion would be Mr. Andrew's alone.

B. What are the options? What would you do in Mr. Andrew's situation?

Development

A. Listen to the song *He's So Fine* composed in 1963 by Ronald Mack and performed by the Chiffons (on the CD, *Greatest Hits of the Chiffons* on EMD/Capitol #36333). Then listen to a recording of the 1970 song *My Sweet Lord* composed by the Beatle, George Harrison (on the CD *All Things Must Pass* EMD/Capitol #46688 or *The Best of George Harrison* EMD/Capitol #46682). You can also listen to them on the internet at the copyright website: www.benedict.com. Did George Harrison steal Ronald Mack's tune? You decide.

B. In the case of Bright Tunes Music Corp. vs. Harrisongs Music, Ltd., 420 F. Supp. 177 (1976), George Harrison was sued for his song *My Sweet Lord*. The plaintiff (Bright Tunes Music Corporation) claimed that Harrison stole their song *He's So Fine*, written in 1963 by Ronald Mack and performed by The Chiffons. Although George Harrison claimed that he did not knowingly appropriate the melody of the Chiffon's song, he lost the suit because the court felt that his song infringed upon the copyright. The court stated:

> His [Harrison's] subconscious knew it [*He's So Fine* and] already had worked in a song his conscious did not remember . . . . That is, under the law, infringement of copyright, and is no less so even though subconsciously accomplished.

In other words, the court felt that Harrison stole the song. Copyright protects the creators from this and other infringements. The © symbol grants the creators (authors, composers, etc.), not the performers, the exclusive right to:

1. reproduce the copyrighted work in copies or phonorecords
2. perform the copyrighted work publicly
3. prepare derivative works, such as arrangements, based on the copyrighted work
4. publicly distribute the copyrighted work
5. display a copyrighted work (such as a painting or sculpture) publicly

As a conductor or teacher, you have the permission to make certain limited copies of works when the copying consititutes "fair use." Certainly when you buy copyrighted music (enough copies or parts for each student in your ensemble), you have permission to perform it without paying any royalties. Fair use refers to unique circumstances that require you to make copies on your own. For instance, you may photocopy a piece of music in an emergency for an imminent performance provided you purchase replacement copies within a reasonable amount of time. That means, if you ordered a solo for a student's college audition and the music has not arrived in time, you may make a photocopy from a library copy. Or, if a student loses music or misplaces it, you may copy another student's music; however, you must purchase copies to replace it.

In the context of your classroom teaching, you make one copy for yourself and one copy for each student of excerpts provided that the excerpts do not constitute an entire unit that could be performable or is more than ten percent of the total work.

You may not copy music that replaces or substitutes for anthologies or compilations of collected works. For example, you cannot create your own music book of excerpts. You may not copy worksheets, exercises, or standardized tests unless the materials specifically say that permission is granted to duplicate. Finally, you may not copy music that is available for purchase. That includes out-of-print works or excerpts from collections, extra parts that are available for sale, music for accompanists, parts from musicals, or scenes from plays.

Recordings are also protected by the copyright law. You may make a single copy of an audio tape or CD of copyrighted music owned by you or your school for the purpose of constructing aural exercises or for a test. You may also record a single copy of a performance by students if it is made for instructional purposes such as evaluation or rehearsal purposes. You may record your ensemble or cut a CD, provided you obtain the necessary permissions from the publishers of the music you intend to record. Sometimes the recording companies do this for you, sometimes they do not. You may make one videotape of the school musical for assessment and evaluation purposes. If you intend to duplicate copies for the cast members, you must obtain permission.

You may not make arrangements, transcriptions, translations of texts, orchestrations, parody lyrics, or simplified published editions. You must apply to the owner of the copyright (usually the publisher) in each of these instances.

On January 1, 1978, a new copyright law became effective. Additional changes in the copyright laws occurred on March 1, 1989. Specifically, the new law states that a work is "fixed" as soon as it is created and appears in a form which can be recognized by someone else. That means writing the work down on paper, entering it into a computer memory, disk or tape, or recording it on audio or video tape. Once the work is "fixed" it is protected by the copyright law. When two copies of the work are sent by the United States Copyright Office to the Library of Congress, it is registered. This includes payment of a fee. Although registration is not required by law, it is a good practice. For works created or "fixed" prior to January 1, 1978, the old copyright law remains in effect; however, for all works "fixed" after 1977, the new law applies. Copyright protection for works fixed on or after January 1, 1978 expires fifty years after the author's death. Copyright for works fixed prior to January 1, 1978 extend for a period of twenty-eight years from the registration and may be renewed for up to seventy-five years from the first copyright registration date. Fines up to $100,000.00 have been imposed on those who infringe upon the copyright law.

For specific questions, it is helpful to contact ASCAP (American Society of Composers, Authors, and Publishers) at One Lincoln Plaza, New York, NY 10023 or BMI (Broadcast Music, Inc.) at 320 West 57th Street, New York, NY 10019. You may also wish to consult a copyright attorney if you are doubtful. You may duplicate the following forms if they are helpful:

STANDARD FORM RECOMMENDED BY:
Music Publishers' Association of the United States, and National Music Publishers' Association, Inc.

■■■■■ REQUEST FOR PERMISSION TO ARRANGE ■■■■■
PART I

INSTRUCTIONS

This form is to be prepared in duplicate. After completing PART I and signing both copies where indicated, forward both to the publisher who will complete PART II of the form and return it to you. If the publisher indicates a payment for the right you request, and if the conditions are agreeable to you, remit the amount to the publisher together with the original copy, which they will have signed, whereupon the agreement will be completed.

To:_____ Date:_____
(Name of Publisher)

_____
(Address of Publisher)

Gentlemen:

We hereby request your permission and non-exclusive license to arrange the following musical composition:

_____

By:_____(words)

_____(music)

(hereinafter referred to as "The Arrangement")

1. The Arrangement will be for_____
(Type of Arrangement)

in_____.
(Number of Instrumental and /or Vocal Parts)

We will produce_____copies of The Arrangement for use and performance only

by our_____.
(Teachers, Students, Members, Congregation, Etc.)

2. No right to record or to reproduce additional copies is granted to us. We understand that if we wish to record The Arrangement a separate license will be required. We agree not to distribute (except for use of copies as provided in Paragraph 1), sell, loan or lease copies of The Arrangement to anyone.

(OVER)

PART II

3. All copies of The Arrangement shall bear the following copyright notice and the words "Arranged by Permission":

   at the bottom of the first page of music of each part of The Arrangement. We will furnish you with a copy of The Arrangement upon completion.

4. We will have The Arrangement made by a person connected with us as our employee for hire, without any payment obligation on your part, and our signature below; together with yours underneath the words "Permission Granted" below shall assign to you all of our right in The Arrangement and the copyright in The Arrangement together with the sole right of registering the copyright as a work made for hire in your name or the name of your designee.

5. Additional provisions (if applicable):

6. In consideration of your permission to arrange, we will pay you $_____ upon the granting by you of the permission requested.

7. This license agreement sets forth our entire understanding and may not be modified or amended except by written agreement signed by both of us.

   Very truly yours,

   _____
   Name of Institution

   _____
   Address

   By:_____

PERMISSION GRANTED:

By:_____
   Publisher

PERMISSION DENIED BECAUSE:

❏ 1. Arrangement available for sale.

❏ 2. Arrangement in process of publication for sale.

❏ 3. May not be arranged because of contractual commitments.

❏ 4. Other:_____

   _____

INQUIRY FORM ON OUT-OF-PRINT COPYRIGHTED MUSIC
Prepared by: Music Publishers' Association of the United States, and
National Music Publishers' Association, Inc.

INSTRUCTIONS

This form is to be prepared in duplicate. After completing the boxed section and signing both copies where indicated, forward them to the publisher who will complete the form and return it to you. If the publisher indicates a payment for the right you request, and if the conditions are agreeable to you, remit the amount to the publisher together with the original copy, which he will have signed, whereupon the agreement will be completed.

To: _____
(Name of Publisher)

Address: _____

_____

I (We) wish to procure _____ copies of your copyrighted publication:

_____
(Title)   (Arrangement)

by: _____

If it is in print:
Please indicate the price per copy here_____

If it is out of print:
A) Do you have plans to reprint it? _____ If so, when? _____

At what price per copy?_____

B) If there are no plans for reprinting I (we) request your permission to have a non-exclusive right to reproduce by photocopy_____copies for use by my (our)

_____
(students, members, congregation, etc.)

As consideration for your permission to do so, I (we) will pay you in advance of making the copies_____ per copy, totalling $_____ .

The copies will be identical to your publication including the copyright notice. The following will be legibly included on the first page of each copy of our reproduction:

"This reproduction is made with the express consent

of_____
(copyright owner's name)

in accordance with the provisions of the United States Copyright Law."

I (We) acknowledge that I (we) are granted no right to sell, loan or otherwise distribute reproduced copies of the publication other than for the use set down above. No other rights of any kind for any other use are included in this permission.

If you do not grant the above permission, will you supply me (us) with_____ photocopies?_____ If so, at what price per copy?_____

_____

By: _____

Accepted and Agreed to: Address: _____

_____

_____ Date: _____

Improvisation

A. What is legal? Answer each question YES or NO:

1. You have purchased the band score and parts for the Holst *Second Suite in F*; however, you are short two flute parts. You decide to photocopy them and purchase replacement pages later. Are you violating the copyright law?

2. You want to do a musical with your fifth grade. You decide on *Annie*. You purchase the score and decide to write your own script. Are you violating the copyright law?

3. In the above situation, you purchase a script and decide to condense it to one hour. Are you violating the copyright law?

4. The arrangement you wish to perform with the choir is permanently out of print. You have one copy and decide to photocopy it for your students. Are you violating the copyright law?

5. The high school music class is studying the symphony. You wish to photocopy the full score of the first movement of Beethoven's *Symphony No. 1* so that each student can follow along as the music plays. Are you violating the copyright law?

6. While surfing the net you find a wonderful article for your general music class. You download a copy and photocopy enough additional copies for your students. Are you violating the copyright law?

7. You wish to perform the "Tonight" quintet from *West Side Story* with your music theatre ensemble. It is not available as a single copy. You purchase a vocal score and photocopy that one selection for your students. Are you violating the copyright law?

8. Your third graders cannot read musical notation yet. To help them learn choir music that you will be teaching by rote, you photocopy word sheets for them to take home and study. Are you violating the copyright law?

9. You make an overhead transparency of "America the Beautiful" for the students to sing at a morning assembly. Are you violating the copyright law?

10. A parent videotapes the school musical and sells copies to the cast members. Are you violating the copyright law?

11. You have the best ensemble in years and decide to cut a CD of Handel's *Messiah*. Are you violating the copyright law?

12. You purchase an arrangement for your jazz ensemble and find that the tenor sax part is too difficult for your student. You decide to simplify it. Are you violating the copyright law?

13. You wish to have your middle school chorus sing Schubert's "An die Musik" from the collection of Schubert songs you have from your college voice lessons. You photocopy enough scores for your choir. Does this violate the copyright law?

14. You want your private trumpet student to learn a piece that is in an anthology you own. Because you will only be using one piece from the anthology, you photocopy it for her. Does this violate the copyright law?

15. You own a great LP recording of Maria Callas singing an aria your voice student is learning. You make one audio cassette of the aria and give it to your student. Does this violate the copyright law?

16. You find a wonderful graphic in a book that you like very much. You photocopy and use it as the cover for your next concert program. Does this violate the copyright law?

17. You copy the logo design of the Broadway show your students are doing onto t-shirts for the cast to wear and to sell at performances. Does this violate the copyright law?

18. Onto your web page you scan a picture of the orchestra taken by a professional photographer at the state contest. Does this violate the copyright law?

[18-Y, 17-Y, 16-Y, 15-N, 14-Y, 13-N
12-Y, 11-N, 10-Y, 9-N, 8-Y, 7-Y, 6-N, 5-N, 4-Y, 3-Y, 2-Y, 1-N]

B. Pretend that you are the composer of a children's musical called, *Handel Christmas with Care*. The publisher supplies a production kit including a director's score, an accompanist's score, twenty-four choral parts, and a pre-recorded accompaniment tape for a nominal fee. The publisher also makes the director's score available separately. One evening, you are flipping the channels on your cable TV and stumble upon a video performance of *Handel Christmas with Care*, presented by a local elementary school. While you are pleased to see your work performed, you investigate and find that the school purchased only the director's score and photocopied all of the other materials in order to save money. Further, they did not obtain permission to videotape or to broadcast the performance. What will be your next move? Take some time to reflect. Jot down some thoughts.

Recapitulation

A. Share your thoughts with your classmates and teacher. Then return to Mr. Andrew's situation. How can he prevent an impending disaster? What is the "right" thing to do?

B. Invite a copyright attorney, a composer, or a music publisher to class. Present Mr. Andrew's case. What are their ideas?

Bibliography

Abrahams, Frank. "A Learning Styles Approach for At-Risk Students." *General Music Today* 6 (Fall 1992) : 22-27.

Althouse, Jay. *Copyright: The Complete Guide for Music Educators*. East Stroudsbourg: Music In Action, 1984.

Atterbury, Betty W. *Mainstreaming Exceptional Learners in Music*. Englewood Cliffs: Prentice-Hall, 1990.

Battisti, Frank L. "Clarifying Priorities for the High School Band." *Music Educators Journal* 76 (September 1989) : 23-25.

Blakeslee, Michael, ed. *National Standards for Arts Education*. Reston: Music Educators National Conference, 1994.

Bloom, Benjamin S. *Taxonomy of Educational Objectives Handbook I: Cognitive Domain*. New York: Longman, 1956, 1984.

Bogen, Joseph E. "The Other Side of the Brain: An Appositional Mind." *Bulletin of the Los Angeles Neurological Society* 34, 2: 49-61.

Bogen, Joseph E. "Some Educational Ramifications of Hemispheric Specialization." *UCLA Educator* 17: 24-32.

Bolman, Lee G., and Terrence E. Deal. *Modern Approaches to Understanding and Managing Organizations*. San Francisco: Jossey-Bass, 1984.

Bradshaw, John, and Norman Nettleton. *Human Cerebral Asymmetry*. Englewood Cliffs: Prentice-Hall, 1983.

Brandt, Ron. "On Teaching for Understanding: A Conversation with Howard Gardner." *Educational Leadership* 50 (April 1993) (7) : 4-7.

Caldwell, John W., and Lori Y. Beardell. *Arts Law*. Philadelphia: Philadelphia Volunteer Lawyers for the Arts, 1997.

Campbell, Jeremy. *The Improbable Machine*. New York: Simon and Schuster, 1989.

Colwell, Richard. *The Evaluation of Music Teaching and Learning*. Englewood Cliffs: Prentice-Hall, 1970.

Covey, Stephen R. *The 7 Habits of Highly Effective People*. New York: Simon and Schuster, 1989.

Csikszentmihalyi, Mihaly. *Beyond Boredom and Anxiety.* San Francisco: Jossey-Bass, 1975.

Curry, Lynn. *Learning Styles in Secondary Schools: A Review of Instruments and Implications for Their Use.* Madison: University of Wisconsin Center for Education Research, 1990.

Dewey, John. *Experience and Nature.* New York: Simon and Schuster, 1958.

Dewey, John. *Art as Experience.* New York: Minton, Balch & Co., 1934.

Edwards, Betty. *Drawing on the Right Side of the Brain.* Los Angeles: J. P. Tarcher, 1979

Elliott, David J. *Music Matters: A New Philosophy of Music Education.* New York: Oxford University Press, 1995.

Elliott, David J. "Music as Knowledge." *Journal of Aesthetic Education* 25 (Fall 1991) (3) : 21-40.

Elliott, David J., and Doreen Rao. "Music Performance and Music Education." *Design for Arts in Education* 91 (May/June 1990) (5) : 23-34.

Gardner, Howard. "Toward a More Effective Arts Education." *Journal of Aesthetic Education* 22 (Spring 1988) : 163-164.

Gardner, Howard. *Frames of Mind: The Theory of Multiple Intelligences.* New York: Basic Books, 1983.

Gerstner, Jr. Louis V. "At Commencement, Insights and Asides." *The New York Times* (26 May 1997) : 10.

Glenn, Carole. *In Quest of Answers.* Chapel Hill: Hinshaw, 1991.

Gordon, Edwin. *Learning Sequences in Music: Skill, Content and Patterns.* Chicago: G. I. A. Publications, 1997.

Gordon, Edwin. *Advanced Measures of Music Audiation.* Chicago: G. I. A. Publications, 1989.

Gordon, Edwin. *Intermediate Measures of Music Audiation.* Chicago: G. I. A. Publications, 1982.

Gordon, Edwin. Manual for the *Intermediate Measures of Music Audiation.* Chicago: G. I. A. Publications, 1982

Gordon, Edwin. "Taking Into Account Musical Aptitude Differences Among Beginning Instrumental Students." *American Educational Research Journal* 7: 41-53.

Gordon, Edgar B. "A Program of Music Activities Outside the School." In *The Thirty-fifth Yearbook of the National Society for the Study of Education: Part II -- Music Education*, edited by G. M. Wipple. Bloomington: Public School Publishing Company, 1936.

Hallowell, Edward M. *Driven to Distraction: Recognizing and Coping with Attention Deficit Disorder from Childhood through Adulthood*. New York: Pantheon Books, 1994.

Jung, Carl. *Psychological Types*. New York: Harcourt Brace, 1923.

Knieter, Gerald L. "Teaching and Learning Philosophy in the Music Education Doctoral Program." *Journal of Aesthetic Education* 25 (Fall 1991) (3) : 259-275.

Kolb, David A. *The Learning Style Inventory*. Boston: McBer and Co., 1976, 1985.

Kolb, David A. *Experiential Learning: Experience as the Source of Learning and Development*. Englewood Cliffs: Prentice-Hall, 1984.

Kozol, Jonathan. *Savage Inequalities: Children in America's Schools*. New York: Crown, 1991.

Krug, Edward. *The Shaping of the American High School: Vol. 2*. Madison: University of Wisconsin Press, 1972.

Krug, Edward. *The Shaping of the American High School: Vol. 1*. New York: Harper & Row, 1964.

Lautzenheiser, Tim. *The Art of Successful Teaching*. Chicago: GIA Publications, 1992.

Leonhard, Charles, and Robert W. House. *Foundations and Principles of Music Education* 2nd ed. New York: McGraw-Hill, 1972.

Lieberman, Marcus. *An Analysis of the Teaching Style Inventory*. Barrington: EXCEL, 1987.

Mark, Michael L. *Contemporary Music Education* (3rd ed.). New York: Schirmer, 1996.

Mark, Michael L., and Charles L. Gary. *A History of American Music Education*. New York: Schirmer, 1992.

McCarthy, Bernice. *About Learning*. Barrington, IL: Excel, 1996.

McCarthy, Bernice. *The 4MAT System: Teaching to Learning Styles with Right/Left Mode Techniques*. Barrington: Excel, 1980, 1987.

McCarthy, Bernice. *The Learning Type Measure (LTM)*. Barrington, IL: Excel, 1994, 1995, 1996.

McCarthy, Bernice. *The Hemispheric Mode Indicator (HMI)*. Barrington, IL: Excel, 1994, 1995, 1996.

McCarthy, Bernice. "Using the 4MAT System to Bring Learning Styles to Schools." *Educational Leadership* 48 (October 1990) (2) : 31-37.

Music Educators National Conference. *Growing Up Complete: The Imperative for Music Education*. Reston: Author, 1991.

Newmann, Fred M. and Gary G. Wehlage. "Five Standards of Authentic Instruction." *Educational Leadership* 50 (April 1993) (7): 8-12.

Noddings, Nel. *Caring -- A Feminine Approach to Ethics and Moral Education*. Berkeley: University of California Press, 1984.

Noddings, Nel. and Paul J Shore. *Awakening the Inner Eye -- Intuition in Education*. New York: Teachers College Press, 1984.

Oehrle, Elizabeth. "African Views of Music Making." *Journal of Aesthetic Education* 25 (Fall 1991) (3) : 163-174.

Piaget, Jean. *Genetic Epistemology*. New York: Columbia University Press, 1970.

Plato. *Republic II*. Translated by Paul Shorey. London: Willima Heinemann, Ltd., 1963.

Plato. *Republic III* Translated by Paul Shorey. London: William Heinemann, Ltd., 1963.

Reimer, Bennett. "Music Education as Aesthetic Education: Past and Present." *Music Educators Journal* 75 (February 1989) (6) : 22-28.

Reimer, Bennett. "Music Education as Aesthetic Education: Past and Present." *Music Educators Journal* 75 (March 1989) (7) : 26-32.

Reimer, Bennett. *A Philosophy of Music Education* 2nd ed., Englewood Cliffs: Prentice-Hall, 1989.

Rico, Gabriele. *Writing the Natural Way*. Los Angeles: J. P. Tarcher, 1983.

Roger, George L. "Why Teach Music? A Historical Overview of Aesthetics." *Update: Applications of Research in Music Education* 10 (Spring/Summer 1992) (2) : 25-29.

Schwadron, Abraham A. *Aesthetics: Dimensions for Music Education*. Reston: Music Educators National Conference, 1967.

Sola, Peter A. ed. *Ethics, Education and Administrative Decisions*. New York: Peter Lang, 1984.

Spring, Joel. *The American School 1642-1996*. 4th ed., New York: McGraw-Hill, 1997.

Spychiger, Maria B. "Aesthetic and Praxial Philosophies of Music Education Compared: A Semiotic Consideration." *Philosophy of Music Education Review* 5 (Spring 1997) (1) : 33-41.

Strike, Kenneth. A., and Jonas F. Soltis. *The Ethics of Teaching*. New York: Teachers College Press, 1985.

Thompson, Keith P. "Integrating Music into the Curriculum: A Recipe for Success." *Bulletin of the National Association of Secondary School Principals* 76 (May 1992) (54) : 47-51.

Tyack, David. *The One Best System: A History of American Urban Education*. Cambridge: Harvard University Press, 1974.

United States National Commission on Excellence in Education. *A Nation at Risk: The Imperative for Educational Reform*. Washington: Author, 1983.

Waterman, Richard A. "African Influence on the Music of the Americas." *Acculturation in the Americas*, Proceedings and selected papers of the 29th International congress of Americanists, edited by Sol Tax, 207-218. Chicago: Chicago University Press. (1949).

Winner, Ellen, Lyle Davidson and Larry Scripp. *Arts Propel: A Handbook for Music*. Princeton: Educational Testing Service, 1992.

Wilkerson, Rhonda M., and Kinnard P. White "Effects of the 4MAT System of Instruction on Students' Achievement, Retention, and Attitudes." *Elementary School Journal* 88 (1988) (4) :357-368.

----

www.idresearch.com   information on copyright
www.benedict.com   the copyright website